DEEDS OF FAMOUS MEN
(DE VIRIS ILLUSTRIBUS)

DEEDS OF FAMOUS MEN
(DE VIRIS ILLUSTRIBUS)

A Bilingual Edition
Translated and edited
by
WALTER K. SHERWIN, JR.

NORMAN

UNIVERSITY OF OKLAHOMA PRESS

Library of Congress Cataloging in Publication Data

De viris illustribus urbis Romae.

    Deeds of famous men.

    1. Rome—Biography.   I. Sherwin, Walter K.,
1939–   ed. II. Title.
PA6379.D25 1972   937'.00992 [B]   72–867
ISBN 0–8061–1027–9

74 - 6841

To

J. B. Titchener

Contents

Introduction[1]

The *De Viris Illustribus*, hereafter referred to as the DVI, is a series of seventy-seven short biographical units covering Roman history from Proca to Pompey. The work is contained in *Sexti Aurelii Victoris Liber de Caesaribus*, edited by Francis Pichlmayr, published in 1911, corrected by R. Gruendel, and reprinted in 1961. Pichlmayr's introduction contains a summary of past scholarship. Little has been definitely established about this puzzling text. The author is not known; the sources of the anonymous author have never been established, despite various investigations; and the date of composition has not been determined. (Schanz in *Müllers Handbuch der Altertumswissenschaft* vol. 8, part 4, section 1, p. 71 (2nd edition 1914), sums up most of the work, and little has been done since his day. See also H. Behrens, *Untersuchungen über das anonyme Buch De Viris Illustribus*, Heidelberg, 1923, and A. Klotz, *Studien zu Valerius Maximus*, Munchen, 1942.) Fortunately, the manuscript tradition has been established by J. B. Titchener and students working under his direction at The Ohio State University. These studies, conducted over a period of more than thirty years, have not been published because Titchener elected to use the materials in a course in textual criticism.

The task of finding the correct stemma was lightened considerably by Titchener's discovery that all existing manuscripts could be traced back to a single archetype.[2]

I repeat here some of his evidence. On page 27, line 22 (references are to Pichlmayr's text), all the manuscripts[3] have *alios duodecim*. *Alios* is clearly wrong and has been omitted by Pichlmayr. At 28, 10, all the manuscripts have *Iovi delicio*, another obvious error, emended to *Iovi Elicio* by Pichlmayr. The most important piece of evidence occurs at 41, 7. The name *Publius Decius Mus* is omitted in all the manuscripts which have instead the reading *Hic Bello* ....

After a common archetype was discovered, the next step was to establish a stemma. There are nine important manuscripts, of which the oldest and most reliable is *V*. There are six other manuscripts of the fourteenth century, *N*, *f*, *L*, *R*, *C* and *S*. Two codices of the fifteenth century (*o* and *p*) are the only ones to contain an additional nine chapters. The following four groups of proofs indicated that three families existed: *V*; *NfLRCS*; *op*.

I *Agreement between NfLRCS against Vop.*

31, 13 callidus *NfLRCS* callide *Vop*
36, 13 obsidione *NfLRCS* obsidio *Vop*
41, 18 cecidisset *NfLRCS* occidisset *Vop*
46, 11 pecuniam Proserpinae *NfLRCS* Proserpinae *om.* *Vop*
54, 12 etholas *NfLRCS* ettonas *Vop*
55, 21 Gneus Manlius *NfLRCS* Gaius Manilius *Vop*

58, 23 Metellus Caecilius *NfLRCS* Caecilius Metellus
    Vop

   II   *Agreement of NfLRCSop against V*

28, 7 Suffetii *NfLRCSop* Fufetii *V*
28, 13 Suffetio *NfLRCSop* Fuffetio *V*
29, 1 Suffetius *NfLRCSop* Fuffetius *V*
35, 2 ad unum *NfLRCSop* ad unum *om. V*
52, 24 Ticinum *NfLRCSop* Vaticanum *V*

   III   *Agreement of op against VNfLRCS*

26, 17 in arcem *op* in Capitolium *VNfLRCS*
26, 21 forum Romanum *op* Romanum forum
      VNfLRCS
27, 15 interregnum esset et *op* esset et *om. VNfLRCS*
27, 25 utiles tulit *op* tulit *om. VNfLRCS*
29, 3 ut rem corrigeret *VNfLRCS om. op*
29, 4 ab Tullo *op* ab *om. VNfLRCS*
35, 21 Tarquinius ... dedicavit (36, 5). *om. op*
38, 21 coegerunt *op* praeceperunt *VNfLRCS*
50, 23 Spolia ... docuit *op* om. vel corrupt. in
      VNfLRCS
51, 10 Simulacrum Matris deum advexit. Templum
     aedificatur, Nasicae, qui vir optimus iudicabatur.
     VNfLRCS
     Simulacrum Matris deum tum templum aedifi-
     catur iudicabatur quasi hospiti datum *op*

58, 25 Achaeos bis proelio fudit triumphandos Mummio tradidit. *op om. VNfLRCS*

68, 1 unde sperni coeptus ptyriasis *op* unde spe receptus
Puteolos *VNfLRCS*

69, 17 Huius ... curavit (70, 2) *om.* op

70, 2 Gaius Iulius Caesar ... periit (74, 18) *om.*
VNfLRCS

IV   *The final category illustrates further the three*
      independent traditions, V; op; NfLRCS:

45, 26 Tarentini *V* Tarentinorum *op* Tarentinis
NfLRCS

46, 18 suorum *V* eorum *op* servorum *NfLRCS*

55, 1 regni relicti a patre *V* regni parte *op* regni relicti
parte *NfLRCS*

55, 10 arciaci *V* acivi *op* Acilii *NfLRCS*

58, 7 quaestore intelleges hostium *V* quaestore suo in
leges hostium *op* questore in leges hostium
NfLRCS

65, 6 via *V* viam *op om. NfLRCS*

Thus the common archetype branches into three di-
rections *V*, *op* and *NfLRCS*. The last group can be further classified, and the results indicate that no codex is
a copy of any other. In addition, *S* on some occasions
demonstrates the influence of the A family (*o* and *p*).[4]

Now that the stemma is established, some additional evidence produced by Titchener may be given as proof of a common archetype. He listed cases where the A family indicated recognition of an error in the archetype and made an error in its attempt to correct.[5] Besides indicating the existence of a single archetype, these examples demonstrate further the independence of A^1 in his efforts to improve the text.

Pichlmayr's text is not sound because he employed the theory of a "best" manuscript, in this case o and p, as the best basis for the text. The 1961 reprint by Gruendel made no advances. This is not to say that o and p did not supply many good emendations, but only that we should recognize them as fifteenth-century guesses. The stemma proves that o and p were highly emended.[6] Unless new evidence is uncovered to indicate that o and p had another earlier source besides the common archetype, the Pichlmayr text of the DVI must be corrected, and the corrections must be based upon this archetype.

The nine important codices mentioned before, that is, the oldest and o and p, are the only ones considered here (the two groups of fifteenth century codices, not direct copies of any codices of the fourteenth century, are not important in establishing the archetype or a critical text). *Pichl.*, indicating the reading selected by Pichlmayr, is referred to whenever he differs from the reading which

I find acceptable. In most instances, Pichlmayr simply followed *o* and *p* (he even includes nine chapters, LXXVIII–LXXXVI, found only in *o* and *p*), but occasionally he selected a reading also found in a later manuscript without acknowledging that fact.

Since all the manuscripts, with the possible exception of *V*, have been corrected, *V* becomes particularly important. Although some errors exist in *V* (these often may be accounted for by the copyist's carelessness), a study of it indicates that in intent and effort *V* is a fairly accurate copy of the archetype.

The basis of a critical text must be the reconstructed archetype; in this there are obvious errors. An explanation is attempted for each error, particularly those where the text is corrupt or the sense of the passage is missing.[7] Factual errors have, in general, not been changed because I believe that in many cases the original author was responsible and therefore the text ought not to be corrected. For example, in section XLII, Hannibal, at the age of eleven, swore an oath against Rome. The manuscript tradition—that is, the archetype—indicates no variant. Pichlmayr, on the basis of the accepted story and some very late manuscripts, changes *undecim* to *novem*.

One also finds inconsistency in Pichlmayr's corrections. For example, in section XXX, Pichlmayr, following *o* and *p*, changes *Gaius* to *Titus* and *Lamam* to

Apulia, yet he does not change *Pontius Telesinus* to *Gavius Pontius*.

Included in parentheses at the beginning of each Latin section is a page and line reference to the 1961 Teubner edition. Brackets within the text draw attention to some special problem.

I wish to thank the Reverend Richard Bober for his valuable advice and criticism.

[1] This is an expansion of my brief note in *Rheinisches Museum* in 1969, in which I discussed the title of the *De Viris Illustribus* according to the manuscript tradition. In that note, I included the stemma of the important manuscripts without any attempt to verify it.

[2] See his article "The A-Family in the Text Tradition of the Anonymous Liber de Viris Illustribus," in *Classical Studies in Honor of William Abbott Oldfather* (Urbana: University of Illinois Press, 1943), pp. 184–89.

[3] We are concerned with only the nine earlier and more important manuscripts:

> V Vaticanus 1917 anno MCCCXXVIII
> o Oxoniensis 131 S. XV
> p Bruxellensis 9755 S. XV
> N Barberinus IV C34 S. XIV
> f   Reginensis Suec. 1494 S. XIV/XV
> L Regina Lat. 1399 S. XIV
> R Rossiano Lat. 395 S. XIV
> C Oxoniensis 147 S. XIV/XV
> S Hispalensis AA 144–50 S. XIV

[4] Consider the following:

> 27, 25 omniaque *VNfRLC* omnia quae gerebat *opS*
> 37, 9   ob egregia facinora *VNfRLC*
>   ob egregia militiae facinora *opS*

39, 14 redigendum et verberandum *opS* et verberandum
om. VNfRLC
50, 13 Is cum adversum *opS* is cum *om. VNfRLC*

The complete stemma follows:

STEMMA
Archetype

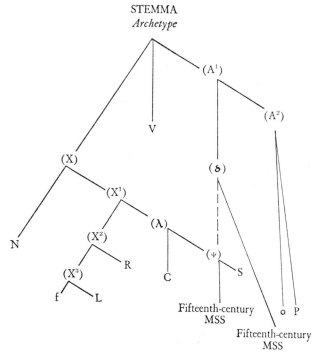

[5] Titchener, *op. cit.*, p. 187.

[6] Stanley Vandersall, in his dissertation (Ohio State University, 1947) *A Mediaeval Editor of the Anonymous De Viris Illustribus*, proved conclusively that *o* and *p* were highly emended.

[7] In some passages, however, there are clearly several word or line omissions which cannot be easily and simply emended.

LIBER DE ILLUSTRIUM
VIRORUM FACTIS

[Gaii Plinii Secundi Oratoris Veronensis *V N f R L C S* Liber Plinii
Veronensis Secundi historici de viris illustribus *o* Haec sequentia
usque ad secundi lib. finem ex. Plinii libro de viris illustribus descripta
sunt *p* (*in margine scriptum*) Incerti Auctoris Liber De Viris Illustribus Urbis Romae *Pichl.* liber de illustrium *V f* liber illustrium
N R L de viris illustribus liber *C S* Liber de illustrium virorum factis
scripsi]

DEEDS OF FAMOUS MEN

I

PROCA,[1] rex Albanorum, Amulium et Numitorem filios
habuit, quibus regnum annuis vicibus habendum reliquit
ut alternis imperarent. Sed Amulius fratri imperium non
dedit et ut eum subole privaret, filiam[2] illius, Rheam
Silviam, Vestae sacerdotem praefecit, ut virginitate per-
petua teneretur, quae a Marte compressa, Remum et
Romulum edidit. Amulius ipsam in vincula compegit,
parvulos in Tiberim abiecit, quos aqua in sicco reliquit.
Ad vagitum lupa accurrit eosque uberibus suis aluit. Mox
Faustulus pastor collectos Accae[3] Laurentiae coniugi
educandos dedit. Qui postea Amulio interfecto Numitori
avo regnum restituerunt; ipsi pastoribus adunatis civitatem condiderunt, quam Romulus augurio victor, quod
ipse duodecim, Remus sex vultures viderat, Romam
vocavit, et[4] ut eam prius legibus muniret quam moeni-
bus, edixit ne quis vallum transiliret; quod Remus irri-
dens transilivit et a Celere centurione rastro[5] fertur
occisus.

1 Proca . . . vultures viderat *om.* p
2 filiam eius *o Pichl.*
3 Accae *fRSo* acte *NLC* arce *V*
4 et . . . legibus *om. p*
5 rutro vel rastro ferreo occisus *o p*

I

PROCA, king of the Albans, had two sons, Amulius and Numitor, to whom he left his kingdom to be ruled alternately one year at a time. But Amulius did not relinquish command to his brother, and in order to deprive him of posterity, appointed Numitor's daughter Rhea Silvia a priestess of Vesta to bind her in permanent virginity. But she was made pregnant by Mars and bore Remus and Romulus. Amulius locked her in chains and cast the little boys into the Tiber. The water left them on dry land. A wolf hurried to their crying and nourished them with her teats. Faustulus, a shepherd, then took them to his wife, Acca Laurentia, to be reared. Afterwards they killed Amulius and restored the kingdom to their grandfather Numitor. They united the shepherds and founded a state which Romulus, victor in the augury because he had seen twelve vultures and Remus six, called Rome. In order to protect it with laws before the fortifications were completed, he forbade anyone to jump across the fortification. Remus, jeering, jumped across, and is said to have been killed with a hoe by the centurion Celer.

Romulus asylum convenis patefecit et magno exercitu facto cum videret coniugia deesse, per legatos a finitimis civitatibus petiit.[1] Quibus negatis ludos Consualia[2] simulavit; ad quos cum utriusque sexus multitudo venisset, dato suis signo virgines raptae sunt. Ex quibus cum una pulcherrima cum magna admiratione[3] omnium duceretur, Thalassio eam duci responsum[4] est. Quae nuptiae quia feliciter cesserant, institutum est, ut in omnibus nuptiis Thalasii nomen uteretur.[5] Cum feminas finitimorum Romani[6] rapuissent, primi Caeninenses contra eos bellum sumpserunt. Adversus quos Romulus processit et exercitum eorum ac ducem Acronem singulari proelio devicit. Spolia opima in Capitolio[7] Iovi Feretrio consecravit. Sabini ob raptas bellum adversus Romanos sumpserunt. Et cum Romae appropinquarent, Tarpeiam virginem nacti quae aquae causa sacrorum hauriendae descenderat, ei Titus Tatius optionem muneris dedit, si exercitum suum in capitolium[8] perduxisset. Illa petiit, quod illi in sinistris manibus gerebant, videlicet anulos et armillas; quibus dolose repromissis Sabinos in arcem perduxit, ubi Tatius scutis eam obrui praecepit; nam et ea in laevis habuerant. Romulus adversum[9] Tatium, qui montem Tarpeium tenebat, processit et in eo loco, ubi nunc Romanum[10] forum est, pugnam conseruit: ibi Hostus Hostilius fortissime dimicans cecidit, cuius interitu consternati Romani fugere coeperunt. Tunc Romulus

II

Romulus opened an asylum for refugees, raised a large army, and, when he saw the lack of marriages, through legates sought these connections from neighboring states. When these were denied, he pretended to celebrate the games in honor of Consus. When a crowd of men and women had come to these, he gave a signal to his men, and young women were seized. When one very beautiful woman was admired greatly by all as she was led away, the response was given that she was being taken to Talassius. Since these nuptials turned out successfully, it was instituted that in all weddings the name of Talassius be used.

After the Romans had seized their neighbors' women, the inhabitants of Caenina were the first to undertake war against them. Romulus proceeded against them and defeated their army and their leader Acron in single combat. On the Capitol he consecrated the choicest spoils to Jupiter Feretrius. The Sabines undertook war against the Romans for the women who were seized. And when they approached Rome, they met with the maiden Tarpeia, who had descended to draw water for the sacrifices. Titus Tatius gave her the choice of a gift if she would guide his army into the capital. She asked for what they were wearing on their left hands, meaning their rings and bracelets of course. When these were deceitfully promised, she led the Sabines into the citadel,

Iovi Statori aedem vovit, et exercitus seu forte seu divini-
tus restitit. Tunc raptae in memoria[11] processerunt et
hinc[12] matres inde coniuges deprecatae pacem concilia-
runt. Romulus foedus percussit et Sabinos in urbem
recepit, populum a Curibus, oppido Sabinorum, Quirites
vocavit. Centum senatores a pietate patres appellavit.
Tres equitum centurias instituit, quas suo nomine
Ramnes, a Tito Tatio Ticinenses,[13] a luci communione
Luceres appellavit. Plebem[14] in triginta curias distribuit
easque raptarum nominibus appellavit. Cum ad Caprae
paludem exercitum lustraret, nusquam comparuit; unde
inter patres et populum seditione orta Iulius Proculus vir
nobilis, in contionem processit et iureiurando[15] firmavit
Romulum a se in colle Quirinali visum augustiore forma,
cum ad deos abiret; eundemque praecipere, ut seditioni-
bus abstinerent, virtutem colerent; futurum, ut omnium
gentium domini exsisterent. Huius auctoritati creditum
est. Aedes in colle Quirinali Romulo constituta, ipse pro
deo cultus et Quirinus est appellatus.

---

[1] petiit *V C S* petit *fRLopN*

[2] consilio sumulavit *L*

[3] omnium admiratione *Pichl.*

[4] responsum est *o* responsum . . . omnibus nuptiis *om. p.*

[5] uteretur *V* iteretur *op* invocaretur *fRL* vocaretur *CNS*

[6] Romani vi *NfRLS Pichl.* vi *om. VCop*

[7] Iovi Feretrio in Capitolio *Pichl.*

[8] arcem *op Pichl.*

[9] adversum *VNRL* adversus *fCS op Pichl.*

[10] forum Romanum *op Pichl.*

where Tatius ordered that she be crushed with their shields; for they had these also in their left hands.

Romulus proceeded against Tatius, who was holding the Tarpeian Mountain, and joined battle in that very spot where the Roman Forum is now. Hostus Hostilius fell there fighting very bravely. Terrified at his fall, the Romans began to flee. Romulus then vowed a temple to Jupiter Stator, and whether by chance or divine providence, the army made a stand. Then the women who were seized left their mark on history as they interceded on this side as mothers, on that as wives, and brought about peace. Romulus struck a treaty and accepted the Sabines into the city. He called the people Quirites after Cures, a Sabine town. One hundred senators he named patres because of their piety. He established three centuries of Equites which he named Ramnes from his own name, Ticinenses from Titus Tatius, Luceres from the participation of the grove. He distributed the people into thirty curias and named them after the women who were abducted. While he was reviewing the army at Caprae Palus, he disappeared. From this a dispute arose between the patres and the people, and Julius Proculus, a noble, came into the assembly and asserted under oath that Romulus appeared to him on Mount Quirinal in more majestic splendor as he was departing for the immortals. Proculus asserted that Romulus instructed them to abstain from seditions and practice virtue, and in this

[11] in memoria *VNC* in medium *fRLSop Pichl.*
[12] hinc matres *VCop* hinc patres *NfRLS Pichl.*
[13] Ticinenses *VNfRLSC* Titiensis *p* Titienses *o* Tatienses *Pichl.*
[14] Plebem . . . appellavit *om. fLCS*
[15] iure *om. VCo*

way they would become masters of all nations. The Romans trusted in his authority. A temple to Romulus was built on the Quirinal; he himself was reverenced as a god and was named Quirinus.

III

(27, 15)

Post consecrationem Romuli cum[1] seditiones orirentur, Numa Pompilius, Pomponii filius, Curibus, oppido Sabinorum, accitus, cum addicentibus avibus Romam venisset, ut populum ferum religione molliret, sacra plurima instituit. Aedem Vestae fecit, virgines Vestales legit. Flamines tres, Dialem Martialem Quirinalem, Salios, Martis sacerdotes, quorum primus praesul vocatur, duodecim[2] instituit. Pontificem maximum creavit, portas Iano gemino aedificavit. Annum in duodecim menses distribuit additis Ianuario et Februario. Leges quoque plures et utiles,[3] omniaque[4] iussu Egeriae nymphae[5] coniugis suae, se facere simulavit.[6] Ob hanc tantam iustitiam bellum ei nemo intulit. Morbo solutus in Ianiculo sepultus est, ubi post annos fercula[7] cum libris a Terentio[8] quodam exarata; qui libri quia leves quasdam sacrorum causas continebant, ex auctoritate patrum cremati sunt.

[1] cum seditiones orirentur *scripsi* cum diu interregnum seditiones orirentur *VfRLCNS* cum diu interregnum esset et seditiones orirentur *op Pichl*.

[2] alios duodecim *omnes codd*. alios *om. Pichl*.

[3] utiles tulit *op Pichl*.

[4] omnia quae gerebat *Pichl. Sop*

[5] nymphae uxoris *Pichl*.

[6] simulavit *scripsi* simulans *omnes codd. Pichl*.

[7] fercula *VNfRCS* arcula *Lop Pichl*.

[8] Tarentio *V* Terrentio *N*

III

AFTER the deification of Romulus, when seditions arose, Numa Pompilius, son of Pomponius, was summoned from the Sabine town of Cures. When he had come to Rome under favorable omens, he instituted many sacred ceremonies in order to tame by religion a fierce people. He built a temple to Vesta and chose Vestal virgins. He instituted three flamens, to Jupiter, Mars, and Romulus and twelve priests of Mars, the Salii, of whom the first is called praesul. He created the office of Pontifex Maximus and built doors to Janus Geminus. He divided the year into twelve months after adding January and February. He pretended that the many useful laws and all the things which he did were at the order of Egeria, his nymph-wife. So great was this righteousness of his that no one brought war on him. He died from an illness and was buried on the Janiculum, where, years later, biers containing books were dug up by a certain Terentius. These books were burned on the authority of the patres because they contained certain trivial causes for sacred ceremonies.

IV
(28, 4)

Tullus Hostilius, quia bonam operam adversum Sabinos moverat,[1] rex creatus bellum Albanis indixit quod trigeminorum certatione finivit. Albam propter perfidiam ducis Metii Fufetii[2] diruit, Albanos Romam transire iussit. Curiam Hostiliam constituit. Montem Coelium urbi addidit. Et dum Numam Pompilium sacrificiis imitatur, Iovi[3] Elicio litare non potuit, fulmine ictus cum regia conflagravit.

Cum inter[4] Romanos et Albanos bellum fuisset exortum, ducibus Hostilio et Fufetio[5] placuit rem paucorum certatione[6] finire. Et[7] erant apud Romanos trigemini Horatii, tres apud Albanos Curiatii; quibus foedere icto concurrentibus statim duo Romanorum ceciderunt, tres Albanorum vulnerati. Unus Horatius quamvis integer, quia tribus impar erat, fugam simulavit et singulos per intervalla[8] interfecit. Et cum spoliis onustus rediret, sororem obviam habuit, quae viso paludamento sponsi sui, qui unus ex Curiatiis erat, flere coepit. Frater eam occidit. Qua re apud duumviros condemnatus ad populum provocavit; ubi patris lacrimis condonatus ab eo expiandi gratia sub tigillum missus; quod nunc quoque viae superpositum Sororium appellatur.

Metius Fufetius,[9] dux Albanorum, cum se invidiosum apud cives videret, quod bellum sola trigeminorum certatione finisset, ut[10] rem corrigeret, Veientes et Fidenates adversum Romanos incitavit. Ipse Tullo[11] in auxilium accersitus aciem in collem subduxit, ut fortunam sequere-

IV

TULLUS HOSTILIUS, made king because of his good work against the Sabines, waged war on the Albans which he ended by the contest of the three brothers. He destroyed Alba because of the treachery of its leader, Metius Fufetius, and ordered the Albans to move to Rome. He established the Hostilian Curia and added the Caelian Hill to the city. And while imitating Numa Pompilius in sacrifices, he was not able to appease Jupiter Elicius. Struck by lightning, he was consumed by fire along with his palace.

In the war against Alba, the leaders Hostilius and Fufetius resolved to finish the affair by a combat of a few. Among the Romans were three brothers, the Horatii, and among the Albans, three Curiatii. After the treaty was made, the brothers engaged in combat. At once two Romans were killed, three Albans wounded. The one Horatius, although unwounded, because he was no match for three, pretended to flee and killed the Curiatii one by one at intervals. Returning laden with spoils he met his sister who began to weep when she saw the cloak of her fiance, who was one of the Curiatii. The brother killed her. Condemned therefore before the duumvirs, he appealed to the people. The tears of his father led to his pardon. For expiation he was sent under the yoke by the people. A beam was placed across the road and is now called the Sister's Beam.

Metius Fufetius, the Alban leader, seeing that he was

tur. Qua re Tullus intellecta magna voce ait suo illud
iussu Metium facere. Qua re hostes territi et victi sunt.
Postera die Metius cum ad gratulandum Tullo venisset,
iussu ipsius quadrigis religatus et in diversa distractus est.

[1] moverat *V N* navaverat *∫RC Pichl.* manaverat *L* noverat *op*

[2] Fufetii *V* Suffetii *N∫RLCop*

[3] Iovi Elicio *Pichl.* Iovi delicio *omnes codd.*

[4] inter Romanos et Albanos *∫RL Pichl.* Romanos et *om. VNCSop*

[5] Fuffetio *V*

[6] certatione *VNCS* certamine *∫Lop Pichl.*

[7] Et (erant) *om. Pichl.*

[8]intervalla interfecit *scripsi* intervalla ut vulnerum dolor interfecit
V N ut vulnerum dolor erat interfecit *∫RLCS* ut vulnerum dolor
patiebatur, insequentes interfecit *op Pichl.*

[9] Fuffetius *V*

[10] ut rem corrigeret *om. op.*

[11] ab Tullo *op Pichl.*

hated by his citizens because he had ended the war by the single contest of the three brothers, tried to correct the matter by inciting the Veientes and Fidenates against the Romans. He himself, called to bring help to Tullus, drew up his battle line on a hill in order to follow the winning side. Tullus understood the situation and shouted loudly that Metius was following his orders. The enemy therefore became frightened and were defeated. On the next day when Metius came to congratulate him, Tullus ordered him to be tied to teams of four horses and torn into pieces.

V

(29, 11)

ANCUS MARCIUS, Numae Pompilii ex filia nepos, aequi-
tate et religione avo similis, Latinos bello domuit. Aventinum[1] et Murcium montes urbi addidit. Nova moenia
oppido circumdedit. Silvas ad usum navium publicavit.
Salinarum vectigal instituit. Carcerem primus aedificavit. Ostiam coloniam maritimis commeatibus oppor-
tunam in ostio Tiberis deduxit. Ius fetiale, quo legati ad
res repetundas uterentur, ab Aequiculis transtulit, quod
primus Fertor[2] Resius excogitavit. His rebus intra paucos
dies confectis immatura morte praereptus non potuit
praestare qualem promiserat regem.

[1] Aventinum et Murcium *VfR* Aventinum et Ianiculum *op* Aventinum et Martium *NS* Aventinum et Murtium *C* Murcium et Ianiculum *Pichl.*

[2] Fertor Resius excogitavit. *Renier* fertur Hessus excogitasse
VNfRLCS fertur Rhesus excogitasse *p Pichl.* fertur Resus excogitasse *o*

V

ANCUS MARCIUS, grandson of Numa Pompilius on his mother's side, similar to his grandfather in fairness and piety, conquered the Latins. He added the Aventine and Murcian hills to the city. He surrounded the town with new walls. He confiscated forests for the construction of ships. He instituted a tax on salt-works. He was the first to build a prison. At the mouth of the Tiber he founded Ostia, a colony suitable for maritime commerce. He adopted from the Aequicoli the fetial right, first devised by Fertor Resius, and used by legates to demand satisfaction from an enemy. These things were accomplished within a few days. Ancus suffered a premature death and was not able to distinguish himself as the king he had given evidence of being.

VI

(29, 23)

Lucius Tarquinius Priscus[1] (Lucumo) graeci Demarati filius qui Cypseli[2] tyrannidem fugiens in Etruriam commigravit. Ipse Lucumo dictus, urbe Tarquiniis profectus Romam petiit. Advenienti aquila pilleum sustulit et, cum alte subvolasset, reposuit. Tanaquil coniux, auguriorum perita, regnum ei portendi intellexit. Tarquinius pecunia et industria dignitatem atque etiam Anci regis familiaritatem consecutus;[3] a quo tutor liberis relictus regnum intercepit et ita administravit, quasi iure adeptus fuisset. Centum patres in curiam legit qui minorum gentium sunt appellati. Equitum centurias numero duplicavit, nomina mutare non potuit Atti Nevii[4] auguris auctoritate deterritus, qui fidem artis suae novacula et cote firmavit. Latinos bello domuit. Circum maximum aedificavit. Ludos magnos instituit. De Sabinis et priscis Latinis triumphavit. Murum lapideum urbi circumdedit. Filium tredecim annorum, quod in proelio hostem percussisset, praetexta bullaque donavit, unde haec puerorum ingenuorum insignia esse coeperunt. Post ab Anci liberis immissis percussoribus per dolum regno[5] excitus[6] et interfectus est.

[1] Priscus Lucumo greci Demarati Corinthii *op* Priscus Demarati Corinthii *Pichl.*

[2] Cypseli *Pichl.* Cypselis *op* Cypsi *N cett. codd. varie corrupti*

[3] consecutus est *op Pichl.*

[4] Nevii *Sp Pichl.* Nevi *R* Navii *L* Nenii *fCo* veni *V* Novi *N*

[5] regia *op Pichl*

[6] excitus *Vop* exutus *NfRLCS*

VI

Lucius Tarquinius Priscus (Lucumo) was the son of the Greek Demaratus, who fled the tyranny of Cypselus and migrated to Etruria. Tarquin himself, called Lucumo, left the city of Tarquinii and sought Rome. At his arrival an eagle snatched his hat, flew high up, and then replaced it. His wife Tanaquil, skilled in augury, understood that the kingdom was signified. Tarquin, by his money and diligence, acquired rank and even the friendship of King Ancus. Named in the King's will as tutor to his children, Tarquin usurped the kingdom and ruled as if he had obtained it justly. He selected one hundred patres for the Senate who were named from the "lesser families." He doubled the centuries of Equites but was not able to change their names, since he was prevented by the authority of the augur Attius Nevius, who strengthened confidence in his art with his razor and whetstone. He defeated the Latins, built the Circus Maximus, instituted great public games, celebrated triumphs over the Sabines and ancient Latins, and surrounded the city with a stone wall. He presented his thirteen-year-old son with the praetexta [toga] and bulla [an ornament] because he had killed an enemy in battle. From this time on, these became the distinctive marks of free-born children. Afterward, assassins were sent by the children of Ancus and, summoning Tarquin from his kingdom by means of deceit, killed him.

VII
(30, 19)

Servius Tullius, (Puri)[1] Corniculanii et Ocresiae[2] captivae filius, cum in domo Tarquinii Prisci educaretur, flammae species caput eius amplexa est. Hoc visu Tanaquil summam dignitatem portendi intellexit. Coniugi suasit, ut eum ita ut liberos suos educaret. Qui cum adolevisset, gener a Tarquinio assumptus est, et cum rex occisus esset, Tanaquil ex altiore[3] ad populum despiciens ait Priscum gravi quidem, sed non letali vulnere accepto petere, ut interim, dum convalescit, Servio Tullio dicto audientes essent. Servius Tullius quasi precario regnare coepit, sed recte imperium administravit. Etruscos saepe domuit, collem Quirinalem et Viminalem et Esquilias urbi addidit, aggerem fossasque fecit. Populum in quattuor tribus distribuit ac post plebi distribuit annonam. Mensuras pondera classes centuriasque constituit. Latinorum populis persuasit, uti exemplo eorum qui Dianae Ephesiae aedem fecissent, et ipsi aedem Dianae in Aventino aedificarent. Quo effecto[4] bos cuidam Latino mirae magnitudinis nata[5] est. Responsum somnio datum eum populum summam imperii habiturum, cuius civis bovem illam[6] immolasset. Latinus bovem in Aventinum[7] egit et causam sacerdoti Romano exposuit. Ille callide[8] dixit prius eum vivo flumine manus abluere debere. Latinus dum ad Tiberim descendit, sacerdos bovem immolavit. Ita imperium civibus, sibi gloriam facto consilioque quaesivit.

Servius Tullius filiam alteram ferocem, mitem alteram

VII

SERVIUS TULLIUS, son of Corniculanus and the captive
Ocresia, was being raised in the household of Tarquinius
Priscus when an appearance of fire encircled his head.
By this sight, Tanaquil understood that the highest gran-
deur was signified. She persuaded her husband to raise
him just as their own children. Servius grew up and was
chosen son-in-law by Tarquin. When the king had been
killed, Tanaquil, looking down upon the people from a
more elevated spot, said that Priscus had suffered a
serious but not deadly wound and had asked that during
his convalescence they obey Servius Tullius.

Servius began to rule as if by entreaty, but he administered his command rightly. He subdued the Etruscans
often; added the Quirinal, Viminal, and Esquiline hills
to the city; and built a rampart and trenches. He divided
the people into four tribes and afterwards distributed the
grain to the plebians. He established measures, weights,
and divisions of classes and centuries. He persuaded the
Latin peoples to imitate those who had built a temple to
Diana at Ephesus and said that they should build a
temple to Diana on the Aventine.

After this was done, a heifer of astonishing size was
born. It was the possession of a certain Latin who learned
in a dream that the greatest power would belong to the
people whose citizen sacrificed that heifer. He led the
heifer to the Aventine and explained the situation to the
Roman priest, who cleverly told him that he first had to

habens cum Tarquinii filios pari animo videret, ut omnium mentes morum diversitate leniret, ferocem miti, mitem feroci in matrimonium dedit. Sed mites seu forte seu fraude perierunt; feroces morum similitudo coniunxit. Statim Tarquinius Superbus a Tullia incitatus advocato senatu regnum patrium repetere coepit. Qua re audita Servius, dum ad curiam properat iussu Tarquinii gradibus deiectus et domum refugiens interfectus est. Tullia statim forum[9] properavit et prima coniugem regem salutavit, a quo iussa turba decedere,[10] cum domum rediret, viso patris corpore mulionem evitantem super ipsum corpus carpentum agere praecepit: unde vicus ille sceleratus dictus. Postea Tullia cum coniuge in exilium acta.[11]

[1] Puri *VfRS* Spuri *op* Pari *L* pira *C* primi *N*

[2] Ocresiae *Pichl*. Occretiae *VR* Ocretiae *fCNS* Ocreriae *L* Ocreatiae *p* Ocreciciae *o*

[3] altiore loco *op Pichl*.

[4] effecto *VNfRL* facto *CSop Pichl*.

[5] nata et responsum *op Pichl*.

[6] illam *om. op* illam Dianae *Pichl*.

[7] Aventinum *VSop* Aventino *NfRL*

[8] callide *Vop* callidus *NfRLCS*

[9] forum *VNfRC* in forum *LSop Pichl*.

[10] discedere *fLop*

[11] acta est *Pichl*.

wash his hands in the running stream. While the Latin descended to the Tiber, the priest sacrificed the heifer. And so by his measured action he sought to obtain the empire for the citizens, glory for himself.

Servius Tullius had one fierce daughter and another mild one. When he saw that Tarquin had sons with like passions, in order to soften the dispositions of all by the differences in character, he married his fierce daughter to the mild son and his mild daughter to the fierce son. But the mild ones either by coincidence or by deceit perished; a similarity in character brought together the fierce ones. At once Tarquin the Proud, prompted by Tullia, called together the Senate and tried to claim his paternal kingdom. Servius heard about this and while hurrying to the Senate House was thrown down the steps at Tarquin's order. He was killed as he tried to escape to his home. Tullia at once hurried to the Forum and was the first to greet her husband as king. Tarquin ordered her to leave the crowd. On her return home she saw her father's body and she directed the mule-driver, who was trying to avoid the body, to drive the chariot right over it. From this that street was called Sceleratus. With her husband, Tullia later was driven into exile.

VIII
(32, 4)

TARQUINIUS SUPERBUS cognomen moribus meruit. Occiso
Servio Tullio regnum sceleste occupavit. Tamen bello
strenuus Latinos Sabinosque domuit; Suessam[1] Pome-
tiam Etruscis eripuit; Gabios per Sextum filium simulato
transfugio in potestatem redegit et ferias Latinas primus
instituit. Lacus[2] in circo et cloacam maximam fecit, ubi
totius populi viribus usus est, unde illae fossae Quiritium
sunt dictae. Cum Capitolium inciperet, caput hominis
invenit, unde cognitum est[3] eam urbem caput gentium
futuram. Et cum in obsidione Ardeae filius eius Lucretiae stuprum intulisset, cum eo in exilium actus ad
Porsennam, Etruriae regem, confugit, cuius ope regnum
retinere tentavit. Pulsus Cumas concessit, ubi per summam ignominiam reliquum vitae tempus exegit.

[1] Suessam *RL Pichl.* Seam *Vf* Deam *op* Scam *NS*
[2] Lacus *NfLC* Ludos *op* Latus *RS* Latis *V*
[3] est *om. op Pichl.*

VIII

TARQUIN THE PROUD earned his name from his character. After Servius Tullius was killed, Tarquin wickedly seized the kingdom. Vigorous in war, however, he conquered the Latins and Sabines. He seized Suessa Pometia from the Etruscans. He reduced the Gabians into his power through his son Sextus, who pretended desertion. And he was the first to establish the Latin festivals. He made lakes in the circus and built the cloaca maxima using the energies of the entire people, and so those ditches were called the ditches of the Quirites. When he began the Capitol, he found a man's head, from which it was recognized that that city would be the head of nations. And when his son raped Lucretia during the siege of Ardea, Tarquin and his son were driven into exile and fled to Porsenna, king of Etruria. Tarquin tried to retain his kingdom with Porsenna's help. Driven off, he withdrew to Cumae where he spent the rest of his life in extreme dishonor.

IX
(32, 19)

Tarquinius Collatinus, sorore Tarquinii Superbi genitus, in contubernio iuvenum regiorum Ardeae erat; ubi
cum forte in liberiore convivio coniugem suam unusquis-
que laudaret, placuit experiri. Itaque equis Romam
petunt. Regias nurus in convivio vel[1] luxu deprehendunt.
Et[2] inde Collatiam petunt. Lucretiam inter ancillas in
lanificio offendunt: itaque ea pudicissima iudicatur. Ad
quam corrumpendam Tarquinius Sextus nocte Collatiam rediit et iure propinquitatis in domum Collatini
venit et cubiculum Lucretiae irrupit, pudicitiam expugnavit. Illa postero die advocatis patre et coniuge rem
exposuit et se cultro, quem veste texerat, occidit. Illi in
exitium regum coniurarunt eorumque exilio necem
Lucretiae vindicaverunt.

[1] vel luxu *Vfop* et luxu *R Pichl.* ut luxu *NLCS*
[2] Et (inde) *om. Pichl.*

26

IX

Tarquin Collatinus, son of Tarquin the Proud's sister, shared quarters with the royal young men at Ardea. When, by chance, a banquet became unrestrained and each one was praising his own wife, they agreed to a test. And so they traveled by horse to Rome. They caught the royal daughters in feasting or luxury, and then they sought Collatia. They found Lucretia in the midst of her maidservants working the wool, and so she was judged the most virtuous. Tarquinius Sextus returned to Collatia at night in order to seduce her and entered Collatinus' home by right of his relationship. He broke into Lucretia's bedroom and overcame her virtue by force. On the following day, she called together her father and husband, related the affair, and then killed herself with a knife which she had hidden in her clothing. They swore an oath for the destruction of kings and avenged the death of Lucretia by banishing them.

X
(33, 6)

Iunius Brutus sorore Tarquinii Superbi genitus cum
eandem fortunam timeret, quam[1] frater inciderat, qui ob
divitias et prudentiam ab avunculo fuerat occisus, stulti-
tiam finxit, unde Brutus dictus. Iuvenibus regiis Delphos
euntibus ridiculi[2] gratia comes adscitus baculo sambuceo
aurum infusum deo donum tulit. Ubi responsum est eum
Romae summam potestatem habiturum, qui primus
matrem oscularetur, ipse terram osculatus est. Deinde
propter Lucretiae stuprum cum Tricipitino et Collatino
in exitium regum coniuravit. Quibus in exilium actis
primus consul creatus filios suos, quod cum Aquiliis et
Vitelliis ad recipiendum[3] in urbem Tarquinios coniura-
rant, virgis caesos securi percussit. Deinde in proelio
quod adversus eos gerebat, singulari certamine cum
Arunte filio Tarquinii congressus[4] se ambo mutuis vulneribus ceciderunt.[5] Cuius corpus in foro positum a
collega laudatum matronae anno luxerunt.

[1] in quam *Pichl.*

[2] ridiculi *VNCS* deridiculi *op Pichl. om. fRL*

[3] recipiendos *op Pichl.*

[4] congressus se *VNfLRCS* congressus est ubi *p Pichl.* congressus
ubi *o*

[5] cediderunt *VRSop* occiderunt *NfLC*

X

JUNIUS BRUTUS, son of Tarquin the Proud's sister, because he feared the same fate which had befallen his brother, who had been killed by his uncle on account of his wealth and prudence, pretended stupidity, from which he was called Brutus. For a joke, he was admitted as a companion to the royal youths going to Delphi, and he carried gold poured in an elder staff as a gift to the god. When the answer was given that the supreme power at Rome would belong to the one who first kissed his mother, he kissed the earth. Then after the dishonoring of Lucretia, he swore an oath with Tricipitinus and Collatinus to destroy the kings. When the kings had been driven into exile, Brutus was made the first consul. He struck his own sons with the axe after they had been scourged with the small rods because they conspired with the Aquilii and Vitellii to bring the Tarquins back into the city. Then in the battle against the Tarquins, he met Aruns, Tarquin's son, in single combat. They killed each other. Brutus' body was placed in the Forum; his colleague gave the funeral oration and the women remained in mourning for a year.

XI
(33, 24)

PORSENNA rex Etruscorum cum Tarquinios in urbem restituere temptaret et primo impetu Ianiculum cepisset, Horatius Cocles, illo cognomine, quod in alio proelio oculum amiserat, pro ponte sublicio stetit et aciem hostium sustinuit,[1] donec pons a tergo interrumperetur, cum quo in Tiberim decidit et armatus ad suos transnavit. Ob haec[2] ei tantum agri publice datum, quantum uno die arari[3] potuisset. Statua quoque ei in Vulcanali posita.

[1] solus sustinuit *op Pichl.*
[2] haec *VNRC* hoc *ʃLSop Pichl.*
[3] arari *NRCS* ambire *op* amovere *V* arare vel arari *ʃL*

XI

Porsenna, king of the Etruscans, tried to reestablish the Tarquins in the city. When he had taken the Janiculum at his first attack, Horatius Cocles (he was given that name because he had lost an eye in another battle), stood on the Pons Sublicius and withstood the enemy line until the bridge was destroyed behind him. He fell with the bridge into the Tiber and in full armor swam across to his men. On account of his actions, he was presented by the state with as much land as he could plow around in one day. A statue to him also was erected in the Volcanal.

XII
(34, 4)

Cum Porsenna[1] urbem obsideret, Mucius Cordus, vir
Romanae constantiae, senatum adiit et veniam trans-
fugiendi petiit necem regis repromittens. Accepta potestate in castra Porsennae venit ibique purpuratum pro
rege deceptus occidit. Apprehensus et ad regem pertrac-
tus dextram aris imposuit, hoc supplicii a rea exigens,
quod in caede peccasset. Unde cum misericordia regis
abstraheretur, quasi beneficium referens ait trecentos
adversus eum similes coniurasse. Qua re ille territus bellum acceptis obsidibus deposuit. Mucio prata trans
Tiberim data, ab eo Mucia appellata. Statua quoque ei
honoris gratia constituta est.

[1] Porsenna rex *Pichl.*

XII

When Porsenna besieged Rome, Mucius Cordus, a man of Roman firmness, approached the Senate. He sought permission to go over to the enemy, and he promised the death of the king. The request was granted. He came into Porsenna's camp and there by error killed an officer clothed in purple instead of the king. Seized and taken before the king, Mucius placed his right hand in the sacrificial fire, exacting this punishment from the culprit because it had struck down the wrong person. When he was dragged from the fire because of the king's compassion, Mucius, as if repaying the favor, said that three hundred men like himself had sworn an oath for the king's death. The king, frightened by this, accepted hostages and gave up the war. Meadows across the Tiber were given to Mucius and named after him. A statue also was erected to honor him.

XIII
(34, 16)

PORSENNA Cloeliam nobilem virginem inter obsides accepit, quae deceptis custodibus noctu castris eius egressa
equum, quem fors dederat, arripuit et Tiberim traiecit.
A Porsenna per legatos repetita reddita.[1] Cuius ille virtutem admiratus cum quibus optasset in patriam redire
permisit. Illa virgines pueros quidem[2] elegit, quorum
aetatem iniuriae obnoxiam sciebat. Huic statua equestris
in foro posita.

[1] reddita est *Pichl*.
[2] quidem *VNfRLCS* que delegit *op* puerosque eligit *dett. Pichl*.

XIII

PORSENNA received among the hostages Cloelia, a girl of noble birth. She deceived the guards and left the camp at night. She seized a horse, which fortune had provided, and crossed the Tiber. She returned because of Porsenna's demands through his legates. Porsenna admired her courage and allowed her to return to her country with the hostages of her choice. She selected pure young boys whose age she knew made them liable to molestation. An equestrian statue to her was placed in the Forum.

XIV
(34, 24)

ROMANI cum adversus Vehientes[1] bellarent, eos sibi hostes familia Fabiorum privato nomine deposcit[2] et profecti[3] trecenti sex duce Fabio consule fuerunt.[4] Cum saepe victores exstitissent, apud Cremeram fluvium castra posuere. Vehientes[5] ad dolos conversi pecora ex diverso in conspectu eorum[6] protulerunt. Atque progressi Fabii in insidias delapsi ad[7] unum occisione perierunt. Dies, quo id factum,[8] inter nefastos relatus. Porta, qua profecti erant, Scelerata est appellata. Unus ex ea gente propter impuberem aetatem domi relictus genus propagavit ad Quintum Fabium Maximum, qui Hannibalem mora fregit, Cunctator ab obtrectatoribus dictus.

[1] Vehientes *VNfRC* venientes *L* vegentes *o* veijentes *p* Veientes *Pichl*.

[2] deposcit *VNfRCSop* depoposcit *LPichl*.

[3] profecti *opS Pichl*. profecit *VNfRLC*

[4] fuerunt *VNRCS* exiverunt *fL om. op Pichl*.

[5] Vehientes *VNC* Veientes *LSop Pichl*. Veihentes *fR*

[6] illorum protulerunt, ad quae progressi *Pichl*.

[7] ad unum *om. V* usque ad unum *op Pichl*.

[8] factum est *op Pichl*.

XIV

WHEN the Romans were at war with Veii, the Fabian family demanded to undertake as their own responsibility the performance of the war. Three hundred and six marched out under the command of the consul Fabius. After many victories, they made camp at the Cremera River. The Veientes, resorting to trickery, displayed cattle in various spots within the sight of the Fabian army. The Fabii advanced and were ambushed and killed to the last man. The day on which this happened was put among the dies nefasti [days on which judgment could not be pronounced nor popular assemblies held]. The gate through which they departed was named Scelerata. One member of the family had been left at home on account of his very young age, and he propagated the family to Quintus Fabius Maximus, who by his delaying tactics weakened Hannibal but was called Delayer by his detractors.

XV
(35, 9)

LUCIUS[1] VALERIUS, Volesi filius, primo de Vehientibus iterum de Sabinis, tertio de utrisque gentibus triumphavit. Hic, quia in locum Tricipitini collegae consulem non[2] subrogaverat et domum in Velia tutissimo loco habebat, in suspicionem regni affectati venit. Quo cognito apud populum questus est, quod de se aliquid[3] tale timuissent, et immisit, qui domum suam diruerent. Secures etiam fascibus dempsit eosque in populi contione submisit. Legem de provocatione a magistratibus ad populum tulit. Hinc Publicola dictus. Cum diem obisset, publice sepultus et annuo matronarum luctu honoratus est.

[1] Lucius Valerius Publicola Volesi filius ille Bruti collega *op*
[2] non subrogaverat *Pichl.* non *om. VNfRLCS* alium subrogaverat *op*
[3] tale aliquid *Pichl.*

XV

Lucius Valerius, son of Volesus, celebrated triumphs first over the Veientes, next over the Sabines, and third over both peoples. He was suspected of desiring a kingdom because he did not substitute a consul in place of his colleague Tricipitinus and because he had a home in a very safe place on the Velia. When he learned this, he complained to the people that they had feared any such thing from him, and he sent men to tear down his home. He even removed the axes from the fasces and lowered them in the assembly of the people. He made a law concerning the right of the people to appeal from a decision of the magistrates. From this he was called Publicola. When he died, he was buried at public expense and was honored by a year's mourning by the women.

XVI
(35, 21)

Tarquinius[1] eiectus ad Mamilium Tusculanum gener-
um suum confugit: qui cum Latio concitato Romanos
graviter urgeret, Aulus Postumius dictator dictus apud
Regilli[2] lacum[3] cum hostibus conflixit. Ubi cum victoria
nutaret, magister equitum equis frenos detrahi iussit, ut
irrevocabili impetu ferrentur; ubi et aciem Latinorum
fuderunt et castra ceperunt. Sed inter eos duo iuvenes
candidis equis insigni virtute apparuerunt, quos dictator
quaesitos, ut dignis muneribus honoraret, non reperit:
Castorem et Pollucem ratus communi titulo dedicavit.

[1] Tarquinius . . . titulo dedicavit. *om. op*
[2] Regilli *fRLS* Reguli *C* Regelli *N* Regellicum *V*
[3] lacum *om. V*

XVI

Tarquin, ejected, fled to his son-in-law, Mamilius of Tusculum, who stirred up Latium and severely beset the Romans. Aulus Postumius, appointed dictator, fought the enemy at Lake Regillus. When the victory was doubtful, the master of the horse ordered that the bridles be removed from the horses so that the attack could not be stopped or called back. In this way they routed the battle line of the Latins and captured their camp. Two remarkably brave young men appeared among them on white horses. When the dictator sought them to honor them with worthy gifts, he did not find them. Thinking them to be Castor and Pollux, he dedicated a temple to them under a common title.

XVII
(36, 6)

Lucius Quinctius[1] Cincinnatus filium Caesonem petu-
lantissimum abdicavit, qui et a censoribus notatus ad
Volscos et Sabinos confugit, qui duce Cloelio Graccho
bellum adversus Romanos gerebant et Quintum[2] Minucium consulem in Algido monte obsidebant.[3] Quinctius[4]
dictator dictus, ad quem missi legati nudum eum aran-
tem trans Tiberim offenderant;[5] qui insignibus sumptis
consulem obsidio[6] liberavit. Quare a Minucio et eius
exercitu corona aurea obsidionali donatus est. Vicit hostes; ducem eorum in deditionem accepit et triumphi die
ante currum egit. Sextodecimo die dictaturam, quam
acceperat, deposuit et ad agri cultum reversus.[7] Iterum
post viginti annos dictator dictus Spurium Maelium
regnum affectantem a Servilio Ahala[8] magistro equitum
occidi iussit; domum eius solo aequavit: unde locus
Aequimelium dicitur.

[1] Quintus *op*
[2] Quintum *VCSop* Quintium *NfRL*
[3] cum exercitu obsidebant. *op Pichl.*
[4] Quintus *op*
[5] offenderant *VfRLS* offenderunt *NCop Pichl.*
[6] obsidio *Vop* obsidione *NfRLCS*
[7] reversus est *op Pichl.*
[8] Ahala *p Pichl.* haala *o* Hala *VNfRLCS*

XVII

LUCIUS QUINCTIUS CINCINNATUS disowned his very insolent son Caeso, who, being branded by the censors, fled to the Volscians and Sabines. Led by Cloelius Gracchus, they waged war against the Romans and blockaded the consul Quintus Minucius on Mount Algidus. Quinctius was appointed dictator. The legates who were sent found him across the Tiber plowing, not wearing his toga. He took up the badges of his office and freed the consul from the blockade. For this reason, Minucius and his army awarded him a golden siege crown. He conquered the enemy, accepted their leader's surrender, and marched him before his chariot on his day of triumph. He laid aside his dictatorship on the sixteenth day after he had received it and returned to the cultivation of his land. Twenty years later, he was appointed dictator again, and he ordered Servilius Ahala, the master of the horse, to kill Spurius Maelius, who was striving for a kingdom. He leveled his home, and thus the place received the name Aequimelium.

XVIII
(36, 23)

Menenius Agrippa cognomento Lanatus dux electus adversus Sabinos de his triumphavit. Et cum populus a patribus secessisset, quod tributum et militiam toleraret, nec revocari posset, Agrippa apud eum: "Olim," inquit, "humani artus, cum ventrem otiosum cernerent, ab eo discordarunt et suum illi ministerium negaverunt. Cum eo pacto et ipsi deficerent, intellexerunt ventrem acceptos cibos per omnia membra disserere et cum eo in gratiam redierunt. Sic senatus et populus quasi unum corpus discordia pereunt, concordia valent." Hac fabula populus regressus est. Creavit tamen tribunos plebis, qui libertatem suam adversum nobilitatem[1] defenderent. Menenius autem tanta paupertate decessit, ut eum populus collatis quadrantibus sepeliret, locum sepulcro senatus publice daret.

---

[1] nobilitatem *Vop* superbiam nobilitatis *ƒRLC* nobilitatos *N* nobilitatis superbiam *Pichl.*

XVIII

MENENIUS AGRIPPA (Lanatus was his cognomen) was elected commander against the Sabines and celebrated a triumph over them. And when the people had withdrawn from the senators because they had to endure a tribute and military service and could not be induced to return, Agrippa addressed them: "Once upon a time the members of the human body, perceiving that the belly remained idle, quarreled with it and refused their service. When they themselves became weakened by that agreement, they understood that the belly received and distributed the food to all the members and they became reconciled with it. In the same way the Senate and the people, like one body, will perish by discord, or will become strong by harmony." The people, persuaded by this story, returned. He established, however, tribunes of the people to defend their freedom against the nobility. Menenius died in such great poverty that the people took up a collection, each giving a quadrans [a small coin] for his burial, and the Senate gave a place at public expense for his tomb.

XIX

(37, 8)

GNAEUS MARCIUS, captis Coriolis urbe Volscorum Coriolanus dictus, ob egregia facinora[1] a Postumio optionem
munerum accipiens equum tantum et hospitem sumpsit,
virtutis et pietatis exemplum. Hic consul gravi annona
advectum e Sicilia frumentum magno pretio populo
dandum curavit, ut hac iniuria plebs agros, non seditiones coleret. Ergo a tribuno plebis Decio[2] die dicta ad
Volscos concessit eosque duce Tito Tatio adversus
Romanos concitavit et ad quartum ab urbe lapidem
castra posuit. Cumque nullis civium legationibus flec-
teretur, a Veturia matre et Volumnia uxore matronarum
numero comitatu[3] motus omisso bello ut proditor occisus[4] est. Ibi templum Fortunae muliebri constitutum est.

[1] militiae facinora *Sop Pichl.*
[2] decio *CSop Pichl.* Dexio *V* decimo *fRL* decisio *N*
[3] comitatu *VCS* comitata *fR om. L* comitatis *op Pichl.* comeatu *N*
[4] occisus est *VNfRLCS* est *om. op Pichl.*

XIX

GNAEUS MARCIUS was called Coriolanus from his capture of Corioli, a city of the Volscians. Because of his noble actions, he was given his choice of gifts by Postumius. He furnished an example of virtue and piety by selecting only a horse and a captive who had been host to him. Consul in a time of scarcity, he took care that the people paid a great price for the grain brought in from Sicily. They were forced by this injustice to cultivate their fields and not engage in seditions. He was summoned, therefore, to court by the plebian tribune Decius, but he withdrew to the Volscians, stirred them against the Romans under their leader Titus Tatius, and made camp four miles from Rome. Although he was not appeased by delegations of citizens, he was moved by his mother Veturia and his wife Volumnia, who were accompanied by a number of women. He gave up the war and was killed as a traitor. A temple was built there to Fortuna Muliebris.

XX
(37, 22)

Fabius Ambustus ex duabus filiabus[1] alteram Licinio[2] Stoloni plebeio, alteram Sulpicio[3] patricio coniugem dedit. Quarum plebeia cum sororem salutaret, cuius vir tribunus militaris consulari potestate erat, fasces lictorios foribus appositos indecenter expavit. A sorore irrisa marito questa;[4] qui adiuvante socero, ut primum tribunatum plebis aggressus est, legem tulit, ut alter consul ex plebe crearetur. Lex resistente Appio Claudio tamen lata; et primus Licinius Stolo consul factus. Idem lege[5] cavit,[6] ne cui plebeio[7] plus centum[8] iugera agri habere liceret. Et ipse cum iugera quinquaginta[9] centum haberet, altera emancipati filii nomine possideret, in iudicium vocatus et primus omnium sua lege punitus est.

[1] filiis *ƒRL*
[2] Licinio *NSop* Licino *VR* Lucinio *ƒLC*
[3] Aulo Sulpicio *RCS Pichl.* Aulo *om. VNƒLop*
[4] questa est *op Pichl.*
[5] lege *RSop Pichl.* legem *VNƒLC*
[6] cavit *VSp* scivit *NƒRLC* canit *o*
[7] plebeio *om. Pichl.*
[8] centum *VƒRLopC* quingenta *Pichl. om. NS*
[9] quinquaginta *VƒRLCNS* quingenta *op Pichl*

XX

FABIUS AMBUSTUS married one of his two daughters to Licinius Stolo, a plebian, and the other to Sulpicius, a patrician. The plebian daughter visited her sister, whose husband, as military tribune, had consular power; and she, unbecoming her, became very frightened when the fasces of the lictor were placed near the door. Laughed at by her sister, she complained to her husband. Licinius, with the aid of his father-in-law, as soon as he undertook the duties of plebian tribune, proposed a law that one consul be elected from the plebians. Although Appius Claudius resisted, it passed nevertheless, and Licinius Stolo was the first to become consul. The same Licinius provided a law that no plebian could have more than one hundred acres of land. And since he himself had one hundred and forty acres, and possessed another one hundred and fifty acres in the name of his emancipated son, he was brought to trial and was the first of all to be punished by his law.

XXI
(38, 6)

Populus Romanus cum seditiosos magistratus ferre non posset, decemviros legibus scribendis creavit, qui eas ex libris Solonis translatas duodecim tabulis exposuerunt. Sed cum pacto dominationis magistratum sibi prorogarent, unus ex his Appius Claudius Virginiam, Virginii centurionis filiam in Algido militantis, adamavit. Quam cum corrumpere non posset, clientem subornavit qui eam in servitium deposceret, et[1] facile victurus, cum ipse esset et accusator et iudex. Pater re cognita cum ipso die iudicii supervenisset et filiam iam addictam videret, ultimo colloquio[2] eius impetrato, cum[3] eam in secretum abduxisset,[4] occidit: et corpus eius humero[5] gerens ad exercitum profugit et milites ad vindicandum facinus accendit; qui creatis decem tribunis Aventinum occuparunt, decemviros abdicare se magistratu praeceperunt[6] eosque omnes aut morte aut exilio punierunt. Appius Claudius in carcere necatus est.

[1] et facile *omnes codd.* et *om. Pichl.*
[2] eius colloquio *Pichl.*
[3] cum *om. op Pichl.*
[4] abduxit et occidit *op Pichl.*
[5] humeris *op Pichl.*
[6] praeceperunt *VNfRLCS* coegerunt *op Pichl.*

XXI

THE ROMAN PEOPLE, unable to bear seditious magistrates, elected decemvirs to write the laws. The decemvirs transferred laws from the books of Solon and published them on twelve tables. But when they extended their own magistracy in a pact for tyranny, one of them, Appius Claudius, conceived a passion for Virginia, the daughter of the centurion Virginius, who was with the army on Mount Algidus. When he could not corrupt her, he instigated a client to demand her as his slave. Their victory would be easy since he himself was both accuser and judge. Her father learned of the affair and arrived on the very day of judgment. When he saw his daughter already judged a servant to Appius' client, he obtained permission for a last conversation with her, led her aside, and killed her. Raising her body on his shoulders he fled to the army and incited the soldiers to avenge the crime. They elected ten tribunes and seized the Aventine. They ordered the decemvirs to resign their magistracy, and they punished all of them by death or exile. Appius Claudius was killed in prison.

XXII
(38, 24)

ROMANI ob pestilentiam responso manante[1] ad Aescula-
pium Epidauro arcessendum decem legatos principe
Quinto Ogulnio[2] miserunt. Qui cum eo venissent et
simulacrum ingens mirarentur, anguis e sedibus eius
elapsus venerabilis, non horribilis, per mediam urbem
cum admiratione omnium ad navem Romanam perrexit
et se in Ogulnii[3] tabernaculo conspiravit. Legati deum
vehentes Antium pervecti[4] sunt, ubi per mollitiam[5] maris
anguis proximum Aesculapii fanum petiit et post paucos
dies ad navem rediit; et cum adverso Tiberi subvehere-
tur, in proximam insulam desiluit, ubi templum ei constitutum et pestilentia mira celeritate sedata est.

---

[1] manante *VNfRLC* manente *S* monente *Pichl.*

[2] Ogulnio *Pichl.* Volumnio *VNfRLCS* Otulino *op*

[3] Ogulnii *Pichl.* Volumni *VNfRLCS* in Quinto Burgoni *p* in Burgoni *o*

[4] pervecti ibi *op* pervecti ubi *Pichl.*

[5] mollitiem *op Pichl.*

XXII

THE ROMANS were suffering under a plague and at the response of the oracle sent ten legates under the leadership of Quintus Ogulnius to summon Aesculapius from Epidaurus. When they had arrived there and were admiring a huge statue, a snake, causing reverence, not horror, glided out of the base of the statue. To everyone's astonishment, it continued through the midst of the city to the Roman ship and coiled up in the tent of Ogulnius. Carrying the god, the legates came to Antium. In a calm sea there, the snake sought the nearest sanctuary of Aesculapius and after a few days returned to the ship. When he was being transported up the Tiber, he leaped down to the nearest island, where a temple was built to him, and the plague ended with astonishing speed.

XXIII
(39, 12)

FURIUS CAMILLUS cum Faliscos obsideret ac ludi litter-
arum[1] magister principum filios ad eum adduxisset, vinc-
tum eum iisdem pueris in urbem redigendum[2] tradidit.
Statim Falisci se ei ob tantam iustitiam dediderunt.
Vehios[3] hieme obsidione[4] domuit deque his triumphavit.
Postmodum crimini datum, quod albis equis triumphas-
set et praedam inique divisisset: die dicta ab Apuleio
Saturnino tribuno plebis damnatus Ardeam concessit.
Mox cum Galli Senones relictis ob sterilitatem agris suis
Clusium Italiae oppidum obsiderent, missi sunt Roma
tres Fabii, qui Gallos monerent, ut ab oppugnatione
desisterent. Ex his unus contra ius gentium in aciem
processit et ducem Senonum interfecit. Quo commoti
Galli petitis in deditionem legatis nec impetratis Romam
petierunt et exercitum Romanum apud Alliam fluvium
ceciderunt, die XVI Kal. Augustarum; qui dies inter
nefastos relatus, Alliensis dictus. Victores Galli urbem
intraverunt, ubi nobilissimos senum in curulibus et
honorum insignibus primo ut deos venerati, deinde ut
homines despicati interfecere. Reliqua iuventus cum
Manlio[5] in Capitolium fugit, ubi obsessa Camilli virtute
servata[6] est. Qui absens dictator dictus collectis reliquiis
Gallos improvisos internecione occidit. Populum Romanum migrare Vehios[7] volentem retinuit. Sic et oppidum
civibus et cives oppido reddidit.

[1] litterarii *Cop Pichl.*
[2] redigendum et verberandum *Sop Pichl.*

XXIII

WHEN FURIUS CAMILLUS had besieged the Faliscans, a teacher led the sons of the leading citizens to him. Furius bound him and handed him over to the same boys to drive him back to their city. The Faliscans, because of such great righteousness, immediately surrendered to him. He conquered the Veientes in a winter siege and celebrated his triumph over them. Afterwards he was charged with using white horses to celebrate his triumph and dividing the booty unfairly. Called into court by the plebian tribune Apuleius Saturninus and condemned, he withdrew to Ardea. Later, when the Senones of Gaul abandoned their fields because of their barrenness and besieged Clusium, a town of Italy, three Fabians were sent from Rome to warn the Gauls to cease their attack. One of them, violating the right of nations, proceeded into battle and killed the leader of the Senones. The Gauls, stirred by this, requested but did not obtain the surrender of the legates. They headed for Rome and slaughtered a Roman army at the Allia River sixteen days before the Calends of August. This day was put among the dies nefasti and called dies Alliensis.

The victorious Gauls entered the city, where they at first reverenced as gods the most noble old men in their curule chairs with the badges of honors, and then, disdaining them as men, slaughtered them. The rest of the young men fled to the Capitoline with Manlius. Camillus' courage saved them from siege. Although absent, he

[3] Vehios *NRLC* Veios *Sop Pichl.* Vehies *V* Veihos *ƒ*
[4] obsidio *Lop Pichl.*
[5] Manlio *VRLSp* Manilio *ƒo* Mallio *N* Maulio *C*
[6] est servata *Pichl.*
[7] Vehios *VƒLRC* Veios *Sop Pichl. om. N*

was appointed dictator. He gathered the remaining force, surprised and slaughtered the Gauls. He held back the Roman people who wanted to migrate to Veii. In this way, he restored the town to the citizens and the citizens to the town.

XXIV
(40, 13)

MANLIUS ob defensum Capitolium Capitolinus dictus
sedecim annorum voluntarium militem se obtulit. Triginta septem militaribus donis a suis ducibus ornatus
viginti tres cicatrices in corpore habuit. Capta urbe auctor
in Capitolium fugiendi[1] fuit. Quadam nocte clangore
anseris excitatus Gallos ascendentes deiecit. Patronus a
civibus apellatus et farre donatus. Domum etiam in
Capitolio publice accepit. Qua superbia elatus cum a
senatu suppressisse Gallicos thesauros argueretur et ad-
dictos propria pecunia liberaret, regni affectati in carcerem coniectus populi consensu liberatus est. Rursus
cum in eadem culpa et gravius perseveraret, reus factus
et ob conspectum Capitolii ampliatus.[2] Alio deinde loco
damnatus et de saxo Tarpeio praecipitatus[3] est, domus
dirupta,[4] bona publicata. Gentilitas eius Manlii cognomine[5] iuravit ne[6] quis postea Capitolinus vocaretur.

[1] confugiendi *Pichl.*
[2] ampliatus est *Pichl.*
[3] praecipitatus *op Pichl.*
[4] dirupta *VNfR* diruta *CSop Pichl.*
[5] cognomen ejuravit. *Pichl.*
[6] ne . . . vocaretur *om. Pichl.*

XXIV

MANLIUS, called Capitolinus from his defense of the Capitoline, volunteered at the age of sixteen as a soldier. Decorated with thirty-seven military gifts by his leaders, he bore twenty-three scars on his body. After the city was taken, it was his plan to flee to the Capitoline. Roused one night by the noise of a goose, he hurled down the Gauls who were climbing up. He was called patron by the citizens and presented with grain. He even received a house on the Capitoline at public expense. He was elated with pride. When he was accused by the Senate of keeping Gallic treasures and with his own money freed those who had been made servants to their creditors, he was charged with designs for a kingdom and cast into prison. He was freed by the agreement of the people. When he again persisted, and even more seriously in the same fault, he was arraigned and moved from sight of the Capitoline for judgment. Condemned, therefore, in another place, he was hurled from the Tarpeian Rock, his house was destroyed, and his property was confiscated. His family made an oath, lest anyone afterward be called Capitolinus (from the cognomen of Manlius).

XXV
(41, 1)

FIDENATES, fidei[1] Romanorum hostes, ut sine spe veniae
fortius dimicarent, legatos ad se missos interfecerunt; ad
quos Quinctius Cincinnatus dictator missus magistrum
equitum habuit Cornelium Cossum, qui Lartem[2] Tolum-
nium ducem sua manu interfecit. De eo spolia opima Iovi
Feretrio secundus a Romulo consecravit.

[1] fidei Romanorum *VNfLRCS* veteres Romanorum *op Pichl.*
[2] Laertem *omnes codd.*

XXV

THE FIDENATES, opposed to allegiance to the Romans, killed the delegation sent to them in order to fight more bravely without the hope of pardon. Quinctius Cincinnatus was sent as dictator against them. He had as master of the horse Cornelius Cossus, who killed their leader, Lars Tolumnius, with his own hands. He was the second after Romulus to consecrate the spoils of honor to Jupiter Feretrius.

XXVI

(41, 8)

Publius[1] Decius Mus bello Samnitico sub Valerio Maximo et Cornelio Cosso consulibus tribunus militum exercitu[2] in angustiis Gauri montis insidiis hostium clauso, accepto quod postulaverat praesidio in superiorem locum evasit, hostes terruit. Ipse intempesta nocte per medias custodias somno oppressas incolumis evasit. Ob hoc ab exercitu civica corona[3] donatus est. Consul bello Latino collega Manlio Torquato positis apud Veserim fluvium castris, cum utrique consuli somnio obvenisset eos victores futuros, quorum dux in proelio occidisset,[4] cum[5] collato cum collega somnio convenisset,[6] ut, cuius cornu in acie laboraret, diis se manibus voveret, inclinante sua parte se[7] et hostes per Valerium pontificem diis manibus devovit. Impetu in hostes facto victoriam suis reliquit.

[1] Publius Decius Mus *om. omnes codd.* Hic bello . . . *omnes codd.*

[2] exercitu *ƒRLSop Pichl.* exercitum *VNC*

[3] corona de quercu quae dabatur ei qui cives in bello servasset obsidionali scilcet aurea quae dabatur ei qui obsidione cives liberasset *VƒRL*

[4] occidisset *Vop* cecidisset *NƒRLCS Pichl.*

[5] tum collato *op Pichl.*

[6] cum convenisset *op Pichl.*

[7] se et hostes *VƒLS* secum hostes *NRC* ad hostes *op*

XXVI

PUBLIUS DECIUS MUS was military tribune in the Samnite War under the consuls Valerius Maximus and Cornelius Cossus. When the army was enclosed in the narrows of Mount Gaurus by the enemy's ambush, he requested and received a garrison, escaped to higher ground, and terrified the enemy. In the dead of night, he himself escaped unharmed through the midst of the guards, who were asleep. The army gave him a civic crown [an award of great distinction] for this. He was consul in the Latin War, with Manlius Torquatus as his colleague. When their camp was located at the Veseris River, each consul learned in a dream that victory would belong to the side whose leader fell in battle. The colleagues compared their dreams and agreed that whoever wing was in difficulty in battle, he should promise himself to the shades of the dead. Publius' sector gave way, and he vowed himself and the enemy to the shades of the dead through the agency of the priest Valerius. He made an attack upon the enemy and left the victory to his troops.

XXVII
(41, 23)

Publius Decius Decii filius primo consul de Samnitibus triumphans spolia ex his Cereri consecravit. Iterum et tertio consul multa domi militiaeque gessit. Quarto consulatu cum Fabio Maximo, cum Galli, Samnites, Umbri, Tusci contra Romanos conspirassent, ibi exercitu in aciem ducto et cornu inclinante exemplum patris imitatus advocato Marco Livio pontifice hastae insistens et sollemnia verba respondens se et hostes diis manibus devovit. Impetu in hostes facto victoriam suis reliquit. Corpus a collega laudatum magnifice sepultum est.

XXVII

Publius Decius, son of Decius, in his first consulship, celebrating a triumph over the Samnites, consecrated the booty to Ceres. In his second and third consulships, he performed many deeds at home and with the army. In his fourth consulship, with Fabius Maximus as colleague, the Gauls, Samnites, Umbrians, and Tuscans conspired against the Romans. He led the army into battle, and when his wing gave way he imitated the example of his father. He called for the priest Marcus Livius, set his foot upon a spear, spoke sacred words, and vowed himself and the enemy to the shades of the dead. He made an attack upon the enemy and left the victory to his troops. His body was buried with magnificence after a funeral oration by his colleague.

XXVIII
(42, 10)

Titus Manlius Torquatus ob ingenii et linguae tardi-
tatem a patre rus relegatus, cum audisset ei diem dictam
a Pomponio tribuno plebis, nocte urbem petiit. Secretum
colloquium a tribuno impetravit et gladio stricto dimittere[1] eum accusationem terrore multo compulit. Sulpicio
dictatore tribunus militum Gallum provocatorem occidit. Torquem ei detractum cervici suae indidit. Consul
bello Latino filium suum, quod contra imperium pug-
nasset, securi percussit. Latinos apud Veserim fluvium
Decii collegae devotione superavit. Consulatum recusavit, quod diceret neque se populi vitia neque illum
severitatem suam posse sufferre.

[1] dimittere *VNRCS* omittere *op Pichl. om. fL*

XXVIII

Titus Manlius Torquatus was sent away by his father to the country because of his limited ability and slowness of speech. When he learned that his father was called to trial by the plebian tribune Pomponius, he made his way to Rome at night. The tribune agreed to a secret conference. Manlius drew his sword, terrified him greatly and forced him to give up his indictment. Military tribune under the dictator Sulpicius, he killed a Gallic challenger, removed his necklace, and put it on his own neck. Consul in the Latin War, he struck his own son with an axe because he had engaged the enemy against orders. He conquered the Latins at the Veseris River when his colleague Decius vowed himself and the enemy to Hades. He refused the consulship; he said it was because he could not endure the faults of the people, nor they his severity.

XXIX
(42, 22)

RELIQUIAS Senonum Camillus persequebatur. Adversum ingentem Gallum provocatorem solus Valerius tribunus militum omnibus territis processit. Corvus ab ortu solis galeae eius insedit et inter pugnandum ora oculosque Galli verberavit.[1] Hoste victo Valerius Corvinus dictus. Hic[2] cum ingens multitudo aere alieno oppressa Capuam occupare tentasset et ducem sibi Quinctium necessitate compulsum fecisset, sublato aere alieno seditionem compressit.

[1] everberavit *op Pichl.*
[2] Hinc *Pichl.*

XXIX

CAMILLUS pursued the rest of the Senones. Valerius, the military tribune, since everyone was frightened, proceeded alone against the huge Gallic challenger. A crow from the east settled on his helmet and during the fighting struck at the face and eyes of the Gaul. The enemy was defeated. Valerius was named Corvinus. When a huge multitude oppressed by debt had tried to seize Capua and had compelled Quinctius to be their leader, Valerius suppressed the sedition by taking their debt upon himself.

XXX
(43, 1)

GAIUS[1] VETURIUS et Spurius Postumius consules bellum adversum Samnitas gerentes a Pontio Telesino duce hostium in insidias seducti[2] sunt. Nam ille simulatos transfugas misit, qui Romanis dicerent Luceriam Apulam[3] a Samnitibus obsideri, quo duo itinera ducebant, aliud longius et tutius, aliud brevius et periculosius festinanti.[4] Itaque cum insidias statuisset, qui locus Ferculae Caudinae vocatur, Pontius accitum patrem Herennium rogavit quid fieri placeret. Ille ait aut omnes occidendos, ut vires frangerentur, aut omnes dimittendos, ut beneficio obligarentur. Utroque improbato consilio omnes sub iugum misit acto[5] foedere, quod a Romanis[6] improbatum est. Postumius Samnitibus deditus nec receptus est.

[1] Titus Veturius *op Pichl.*

[2] seducti *NfRLS* inducti *p Pichl.* deducti *Co* selducti *V*

[3] Apulam *op Pichl.* apud Lamam *VfRLCS* apud Laniam *N*

[4] festinanti *VN* festinantibus *fRLCS* Festinatio brevius eligi *op* Festinatio brevius eligit *Pichl.*

[5] acto foedere *V* icto foedere *op Pichl.* ac foedere *N* ex foedere *fRLCS*

[6] Romanis postea *op Pichl.*

XXX

GAIUS VETURIUS and Spurius Postumius, consuls waging war against the Samnites, were led into an ambush by Pontius Telesinus, leader of the enemy. He sent men pretending to be deserters to tell the Romans that Luceria in Apulia was besieged by the Samnites. Two routes led there, one longer and safer, the other shorter for a person in haste and more dangerous. Pontius therefore set an ambush (the place is called Furculae Caudinae) and afterward summoned Herennius, his father, and asked what should be done. Herennius said that either all the men should be killed, so that their strength would be broken, or that all should be released, so that they would be bound by the favor. Pontius disapproved both plans and sent all the Romans under the yoke when a treaty was drawn up and rejected by the Romans. Postumius was surrendered to the Samnites but was not received by them.

XXXI
(43, 15)

Lucius Papirius, velocitate[1] Cursor, cum consulem se adversis ominibus adversus[2] Samnitas[3] progressum esse sensisset, ad auspicia repetenda Romam regressus edixit Fabio Rullo, quem exercitui praeponebat, ne manum cum hoste consereret. Sed ille opportunitate ductus pugnavit. Reversus[4] eum securi ferire voluit; ille in urbem confugit nec supplicem tribuni tuebantur. Deinde pater lacrimis populus precibus veniam impetrarunt. Papirius de Samnitibus triumphavit. Idem[5] Praenesti[6] cum praetorem gravissime increpuisset: "Expedi," inquit, "lictor, secures." Et cum eum metu mortis attonitum vidisset, incommodam ambulantibus radicem excidi iussit.

[1] a velocitate *op Pichl.*
[2] adversus *VfRLC* adversum *NSop Pichl.*
[3] Samnitas *VNfLC* Samnites *RSop Pichl.*
[4] Reversus Papirius securi eum ferire *op Pichl.*
[5] Idem *VLop* Item *NfRCS*
[6] Praenesti *VfRS* Praenestinum *op* pronosticum *C* Praeneste *L* cum Praenestinum praetorem *Pichl.*

72

XXXI

Lucius Papirius, called Cursor (Runner) because of his speed, when he felt that he, as consul, had proceeded against the Samnites with unfavorable omens, returned to Rome to repeat the auspices. He placed Fabius Rullus in charge of the army and instructed him not to engage in combat with the enemy. But Fabius was persuaded by opportunity and engaged in battle. Papirius on his return wanted to strike him with the axe, but Fabius fled to the city. The tribunes did not protect the suppliant. The tears of his father and the entreaties of the people then obtained mercy for him. Papirius celebrated a triumph over the Samnites. The same Papirius at Praeneste reproved a praetor very severely and said "Lictor, prepare the axes." Papirius watched him become terrified by fear of death, and then ordered a root cut out which was in the path of walkers.

XXXII
(44, 3)

QUINTUS FABIUS RULLUS, primus ex ea familia ob virtutem Maximus, magister equitum a Papirio[1] securi paene percussus, primum de Apulis et Nucerinis, iterum de Samnitibus, tertio de Gallis, Umbris, Marsis atque Tuscis triumphavit. Censor libertinos tribubus amovit. Iterum censor fieri noluit dicens non esse ex usu rei publicae eosdem censores saepius fieri. Hic primus instituit, uti equites Romani Idibus Quintilibus ab aede Honoris equis insidentes in Capitolium transirent. Mortuo huic tantum aeris populi liberalitate congestum est, ut inde filius viscerationem et epulas[2] publice daret.

[1] Papirio ob Samnitem victoriam securi *op Pichl.*
[2] epulum *op Pichl.*

XXXII

BECAUSE of his courage, Quintus Fabius Rullus was the first from his family to receive the name Maximus. As master of the horse and almost struck with the axe by Papirius, he celebrated triumphs at first over the Appulians and Nucerians, next over the Samnites, and thirdly over the Gauls, Umbrians, Marsians, and Tuscans. As censor, he removed the sons of freedmen from the list of tribes. He refused to become censor a second time, with the statement that it was not in the best interest of the republic that the same men be made censors too often. He was the first to establish the tradition of the Roman knights mounted on horse parading from the Temple of Honor to the Capitol on the Ides of July. At his death, so much money was accumulated through the generosity of the people that his son distributed meat and provided a feast for the people from this sum.

XXXIII

(44, 15)

Marcus Curius Dentatus primo de Samnitibus triumphavit, quos usque ad mare superum perpacavit. Regressus in contione ait: "Tantum agri cepi, ut solitudo futura fuerit, nisi tantum hominum cepissem; tantum porro hominum cepi, ut fame perituri fuerint, nisi tantum agri cepissem." Iterum de Sabinis triumphavit. Tertio de Lucanis ovans urbem introiit. Pyrrhum Epirotam Italia expulit. Quaterna dena agri iugera viritim populo divisit. Sibi[1] deinde constituit dicens neminem esse debere, cui non tantum sufficeret. Legatis Samnitum aurum offerentibus cum ipse in foco rapas torreret: "Malo[2] hoc[3] in fictilibus meis esse et aurum habentibus imperare." Cum interversae pecuniae argueretur, cadum[4] ligneum, quo uti ad sacrificia consueverat, in medium protulit iuravitque se nihil amplius de praeda hostili domum suam convertisse. Aquam deinde[5] Anienem de manubiis[6] hostium in urbem induxit. Tribunus plebis patres auctores fieri coegit comitiis, quibus plebeius magistratus[7] creabatur.[8] Ob haec merita domus ei apud Tiphatam et agri iugera quingenta[9] publice data.

---

[1] Sibi deinde constituit *VNfRLCS* Idem constituit *op* Sibi deinde totidem constituit *Pichl.*

[2] Malo, inquit *fRLCop Pichl.* inquit *om. VNS*

[3] hoc *VNop* haec *RS Pichl. om. fLC*

[4] gutum ligneum *op Pichl.*

[5] deinde *om. op Pichl.*

[6] de manubiis *p Pichl.* manibus *VNfRLCS* de manibus *o*

[7] plebei *op Pichl.*   [8] creabantur *op Pichl.*

[9] quingenta *VNRS Pichl.* quinquaginta *fLCop*

XXXIII

Marcus Curius Dentatus celebrated a triumph for the first time over the Samnites, whom he pacified even to the Adriatic Sea. On his return he spoke in the assembly: "I took so much land that the area would be desolate if I had not taken so many men; furthermore I took so many men that they would perish from hunger if I had not taken so much land." His second triumph was over the Sabines. As his third triumph, for his victory over the Lucanians, he received an ovation upon entering the city. He drove Pyrrhus of Epirus from Italy. He distributed land among the people giving forty acres to each individual. He then established the same for himself, saying that there should be no one for whom that much was not sufficient. When the envoys of the Samnites offered him gold as he was cooking turnips in his fireplace, he said: "I prefer to eat this in my earthen vessels and to command those who have gold." When he was accused of embezzling money, he brought into their midst a wooden jar which he had customarily used for sacrifices. He swore that he had moved nothing more to his house from the enemy spoils. He used the money from the sale of enemy booty to convey the waters of the Anio to the city. As plebian tribune, he forced the senators to approve the comitia at which a plebian magistrate was elected. Because of his merits, a house at Tiphata and five hundred acres of land were given to him at public expense.

XXXIV
(45, 5)

APPIUS CLAUDIUS CAECUS in censura libertinos quoque in senatum legit. Epulandi decantandique[1] ius tibicinibus in publico ademit. Duae familiae ad Herculis sacra sunt destinatae, scilicet[2] Potitiorum et Pinariorum. Potitios Herculis sacerdotes pretio corrupit, ut sacra Herculanea[3] servos publicos edocerent: unde caecatus est, gens Potitiorum funditus periit. Ne consulatus cum plebeiis communicaretur, acerrime restitit. Ne Fabius solus ad bellum mitteretur, contradixit. Sabinos, Samnitas, Etruscos bello domuit. Viam usque Brundisium lapidibus[4] stravit, unde illa Appia.[5] Aquam Anienem in urbem induxit. Censuram solus omnium quinquennio obtinuit. Cum de pace Pyrrhi ageretur et gratia potentum per legatum Cineam pretio quaereretur, senex et caecus lectica in senatum latus turpissimas condiciones magnifica oratione discussit.

[1] cantandique *op Pichl.*
[2] scilicet *om. op Pichl.*
[3] Herculea *Pichl.*
[4] lapide *op Pichl.*
[5] Appia dicitur. *op Pichl.*

XXXIV

IN HIS CENSORSHIP, Appius Claudius Caecus selected for
the Senate even the sons of freedmen. He deprived flute-
players of the right of banqueting and playing in public.
Two families, namely the Potitii and the Pinarii, were
appointed for the rites of Hercules. Appius Claudius
bribed the priests of Hercules from the Potitii to reveal
the sacred rites to public slaves. Because of this, he was
blinded and the family of Potitii perished completely.
He very bitterly resisted sharing the office of consul with
the plebians. He opposed sending Fabius alone to war.
He conquered the Sabines, Samnites, and Etruscans. He
paved a road to Brundisium, which was consequently
called the Appian Way. He conveyed the waters of the
Anio to the city. He was censor alone for a five-year
period. When discussions of peace with Pyrrhus took
place and Pyrrhus tried to bribe the leading citizens
through his legate Cineas, Appius Claudius, an old man,
blind, carried into the Senate on a litter, denounced
severely these very disgraceful terms in a magnificent
oration.

XXXV
(45, 21)

PYRRHUS, rex Epirotarum, materno genere ab Achille, paterno Hercule[1] oriundus, cum imperium orbis agitaret[2] et Romanos potentes videret, Apollinem de bello consuluit. Ille ambigue respondit: "Aio te, Aeacida, Romanos vincere posse." Hoc dicto in voluntatem tracto auxilio Tarentinis[3] bellum Romanis intulit. Laevinum[4] consulem apud Heracleam elephantorum novitate turbavit. Cumque Romanos adversis vulneribus occisos videret: "Ego," inquit, "talibus militibus brevi orbem terrarum subigere potuissem." Amicis gratulantibus: "Quid mihi cum tali victoria," inquit, "ubi exercitus robur amittam?" Ad vicesimum ab urbe lapidem castra posuit; captivos Fabricio gratis reddidit. Viso Laevini exercitu eandem sibi ait adversum Romanos, quam Herculi adversum hydram, fuisse fortunam. A Curio et Fabricio superatus Tarentum refugit, in Siciliam traiecit. Mox in Italiam Locros regressus pecuniam[5] avehere tentavit, sed ea naufragio elata[6] est. Tum in Graeciam regressus, dum Argos oppugnaret, ictu tegulae prostratus est. Corpus ad Antigonum regem Macedoniae relatum magnifice sepultum.[7]

---

[1] ab Hercule *p Pichl.* ab Herculis *o*

[2] agitaret *V* agitans *NfRLC* agitaret et *Sop Pichl.*

[3] Tarentinis *NfRLCS* Tarentini *V* Tarentinorum *op Pichl.*

[4] Laevinum *NRCS Pichl.* Laevinium *Vop* Laevicium *f* Laevicum *L*

[5] pecuniam Proserpinae *NfRLCS Pichl.* Proserpinae *om. Vop*

XXXV

Pyrrhus, King of Epirus, was a descendant of Achilles on his mother's side and Hercules on his father's side. When he was considering command of the world and saw that the Romans were powerful, he consulted Apollo about war. The oracle responded ambiguously: "Aio te, Aeacida, Romanos vincere posse." ("I say that you can defeat the Romans," or "I say that the Romans can defeat you.") Pyrrhus interpreted this as he wanted and made war upon the Romans to assist the Tarentines. At Heraclea he confused the consul Laevinus with a new tactic—elephants. And when he saw the Romans die with wounds on the front of their bodies, he said: "With such soldiers I could have conquered the world in a short time." When his friends congratulated him, he said: "What value is such a victory to me when I lose the flower of my army?"

He made camp twenty miles from Rome. He returned captives without ransom to Fabricius. When he saw the army of Laevinus, he said that his situation against the Romans was the same as Hercules' against the hydra. He was defeated by Curius and Fabricius, fled to Tarentum, and crossed over to Sicily. Later he returned to Locri in Italy and tried to take away money, but it was carried away by shipwreck. Then, returning to Greece in battle

[6] relata est *op Pichl.*

[7] Pyrrhus cum secundo proelio a Romanis esset pulsus Tarentum, interiecto anno contra Pyrrhum Fabricius missus est, qui prius inter legatos sollicitari non poterat quarta regni parte promissa. Tunc cum vicina castra ipse et rex haberent, medicus Pyrrhi nocte ad eum venit promittens se Pyrrhum veneno occisurum, si sibi quidquam pollicitaretur; quem Fabricius vinctum reduci iussit ad dominum Pyrrhoque dici, quae contra caput eius medicus spopondisset. Tum rex admiratus eum dixisse fertur: ille est Fabricius, qui difficilius ab honestate, quam sol a suo cursu averti posset *op*

against Argos, he was struck by roof-tile and killed. His body was brought back to Antigonus, King of Macedonia, and he was given a magnificent funeral.

XXXVI
(46, 16)

Vulsinii,[1] Etruriae nobile oppidum, luxuria paene perierunt. Nam cum temere servos manumitterent, dum[2] in curiam legerent, consensu servorum[3] oppressi. Cum multa indigna paterentur, clam[4] Romae auxilium petierunt, missusque Decius Mus libertinos omnes aut in carcere necavit aut dominis in servitute[5] restituit.

[1] Item Vulsinia *op*
[2] dein curiam *p* deinde curiam *o* dein in curiam *Pichl.*
[3] servorum *NfRLCS* suorum *V* eorum *op Pichl.*
[4] clam a Roma *op Pichl.*
[5] servitutem *CSop Pichl.*

XXXVI

VULSINII, a famous city of Etruria, nearly perished from extravagance. For when the city rashly freed its slaves, and while it was admitting them to the Senate, it was oppressed by an alliance of the slaves. When the city suffered many harsh things, Rome's aid was sought secretly. Decius Mus was sent and either killed in prison all of the sons of the freedmen or restored them to the service of their masters.

XXXVII
(47, 1)

Appius Claudius victis Vulsinensibus[1] cognomento Audax frater Caeci fuit. Consul ad Mamertinos liberandos missus est,[2] quorum arcem Carthaginenses[3] et Hiero rex Syracusanus obsidebant. Primo ad explorandos hostes fretum piscatoria nave traiecit et cum duce Carthaginensium[4] egit, ut praesidium arce duceret.[5] Regium regressus quinqueremem hostium copiis pedestribus cepit: ea[6] legionem in Siciliam traduxit. Carthaginenses[7] Messana expulit. Hieronem proelio apud Syracusas in deditionem accepit, qui eo periculo territus Romanorum amicitiam petiit iisque postea fidelissimus fuit.

[1] Vulsiniensibus Gaudex dictus *op* Vulsiniensibus cognomento Caudex dictus *Pichl.*

[2] est *om. op Pichl.*

[3] Carthaginienses *Pichl.*

[4] Carthaginiensium *p Pichl.*

[5] duceret *Vop* deduceret *N Pichl.* deducerent *fRLCS*

[6] ea legionem *Pichl.* falagionem *VNfRLCS* eoque legionem *o* eaque legationem *p*

[7] Carthaginienses *p Pichl.*

XXXVII

Appius Claudius, the brother of Caecus, victorious over the Vulsinians, received the cognomen Audax. As consul, he was sent to free the Mamertines, whose citadel the Carthaginians and King Hiero of Syracuse were besieging. First of all, he crossed the strait on a fishing boat to spy on the enemy, and he discussed with the Carthaginian leader the lifting of the siege. He returned to Rhegium and seized an enemy quinquereme [vessel having five banks of oars] with his infantry troops. The quinquereme transported his legion across into Sicily. He drove the Carthaginians from Messana. He accepted the surrender of Hiero in battle near Syracuse. Hiero, frightened by this danger, sought the friendship of the Romans and afterward was a very faithful ally.

XXXVIII
(47, 13)

Gnaeus Duillius[1] primo Punico bello dux contra
Carthaginenses[2] missus, cum videret eos multum mari
posse, classem[3] magis validam quam fabre[4] fecit et manus
ferreas cum irrisu hostium primus instituit; qui[5] inter
pugnandum hostium naves apprehendit, qui victi et capti
sunt. Himilco dux classis Carthaginem fugit et a senatu
quaesivit quid faciendum censerent. Omnibus ut pug-
naret acclamantibus: "Feci," inquit, "et victus sum." Sic
poenam crucis effugit; nam apud Poenos dux male re
gesta puniebatur. Duillio[6] concessum est, ut praelucente
funali et praecinente tibicine a cena publice rediret.

[1] Duellius *op Pichl.*

[2] Carthaginienses *p Pichl.*

[3] classem magis validam quam *VNL* classem validam *p Pichl.*
classem validam quam *o* classem validam quam decorem *S* classem
validam quam decoram *ʃRC*

[4] fabricavit *ʃL*

[5] qui inter *VNʃRLC* sic inter *Sop Pichl.*

[6] Duellio *op Pichl.*

XXXVIII

GNAEUS DUILLIUS was a leader sent against Carthage in the first Punic War. Seeing that Carthage was a great sea-power, he built a strong fleet rather than a skillfully-made one and was the first to provide it with grappling irons, which the enemy mocked. In the fighting, he seized hold of the enemy ships, which were defeated and captured. Himilco, leader of the fleet, fled to Carthage and asked the Senate what they thought ought to be done. When all the senators shouted to him to fight, he said, "I have fought and lost." In this way he escaped the penalty of the cross, for the Carthaginians punished any leader when the situation went badly. Duillius was granted the privilege of returning from a banquet preceded by a flaming torch and a flute-player provided at public expense.

XXXIX
(47, 25)

ATILIUS CALATINUS, dux adversum Carthaginenses[1] missus, maximis[2] et munitissimis civitatibus Henna[3] Drepano Lilybaeo hostilia praesidia deiecit. Panormum cepit. Totamque Siciliam pervagatus paucis navibus magnam hostium classem duce Hamilcare superavit. Sed cum ad Cecinam[4] ab hostibus obsessam festinaret, a Poenis in angustiis clausus est, ubi tribunus militum Calpurnius Flamma acceptis trecentis[5] in superiorem locum evasit, consulem liberavit; ipse cum trecentis pugnans cecidit. Et[6] postea ab Atilio semianimis inventus et sanatus magno postea terrori[7] hostibus fuit. Atilius gloriose triumphavit.

[1] Carthaginienses *p Pichl.*

[2] ex maximis *op Pichl.*

[3] Enna Drepano *Pichl.* Hernadrepano *Vp* Hernadeprano *o* Ethna Drepano *NfRLCS*

[4] Cathynam *p* Cathinam *o* Catinam *Pichl.*

[5] trecentis sociis *op Pichl.*

[6] et postea *VNfRLCS* et *om. op Pichl.*

[7] terrori *om. NfRLC*

XXXIX

ATILIUS CALATINUS, sent as leader against the Carthaginians, drove out enemy garrisons from the largest and most fortified states: Henna, Drepanum, and Lilybaeum. He took Panormus. Roaming about over all Sicily, he overcame with few ships the great enemy fleet commanded by Hamilcar. But when he hurried to Caecina, which was besieged by the enemy, he was enclosed in a strait by the Carthaginians. Calpurnius Flamma, the military tribune, took three hundred men, reached higher ground, and freed the consul. He himself fell fighting with the three hundred men. Later, found half-dead by Atilius and restored to health, he was thereafter a great terror to the enemy. Atilius celebrated a glorious triumph.

XL
(48, 11)

Marcus Atilius Regulus consul fusis Sallentinis triumphavit primusque Romanorum ducum in Africam classem traiecit. Ea[1] quassata de Hamilcare naves longas tres et sexaginta accepit.[2] Oppida ducenta et hominum ducenta milia cepit. Absente eo coniugi eius et liberis ob paupertatem sumptus publice dati. Mox arte Xanthippi Lacedaemonii mercenarii militis captus in carcerem missus. Legatus de permutandis captivis Romam missus dato iureiurando, ut si[3] non impetrasset, ita demum rediret, in senatu condicionem dissuasit reiectisque a[4] se coniuge et liberis Carthaginem regressus, ubi in arcam ligneam coniectus clavis introrsum adactis vigiliis ac dolore punitus est.

[1] Ea quassata *op Pichl.* Aquassata *VNRCS* conquassatas *L* aquassatas ∫

[2] cepit *op Pichl.*

[3] si impetrasset, ita demum non rediret *op Pichl.*

[4] a se *V∫RLNCS* ab amplexu *op Pichl.*

XL

MARCUS ATILLIUS REGULUS celebrated a triumph as consul because of his rout over the Sallentines. He was the first of the Roman leaders to cross a fleet to Africa. With a battered fleet he captured sixty-three warships from Hamilcar. He took two hundred towns and 200,000 men. During his absence, public funds were given to his wife and children on account of their poverty. Later, he was captured through the skill of Xanthippus, a mercenary soldier from Sparta, and sent to prison. He was sent as a legate to Rome about exchanging captives after he swore an oath to return if he did not achieve success. He argued against the agreement in the Senate, pushed away his wife and children, and returned to Carthage. He was thrown into a wooden box into which nails were driven, and he was punished with sleeplessness and pain.

XLI
(48, 24)

QUINTUS LUTATIUS CATULUS primo Punico bello trecentis navibus adversum Poenos profectus sexcentas eorum naves commeatibus et aliis oneribus impeditas duce[1] Himilcone apud Aegates[2] insulas inter Siciliam et Africam depressit aut cepit finemque bello imposuit. Pacem petentibus hac condicione concessit, ut Sicilia, Sardinia et ceteris insulis inter Italiam Africamque decederent, Hispania citra Hiberum abstinerent.

[1] duce Hannone *op Pichl.*
[2] Egates *NfRLC* Egatas *S* Esadas *V* Egadas *op* Aegatas *Pichl.*

XLI

In the First Punic War, Quintus Lutatius Catulus set
out with three hundred ships against the Carthaginians.
At Aegates Insulae, between Sicily and Africa, against
Himilco, he sunk or captured six hundred of their ships
loaded with supplies and other cargo and ended the war.
They sought peace, and he granted it, with the condition
that they leave Sicily, Sardinia, and other islands between
Italy and Africa and stay away from Spain on this side
of the Iberus River.

XLII
(49, 5)

HANNIBAL, Hamilcaris filius, undecim[1] annos natus, a patre aris admotus odium in Romanos perenne iuravit. Exinde socius et miles in castris patri fuit. Mortuo eo causam belli quaerens Saguntum Romanis foederatam intra sex menses evertit. Tum Alpibus patefactis in Italiam traiecit. Publium Scipionem apud Ticinum Sempronium Longum apud Cremeram,[2] Flaminium apud Trasimenum, Paullum et Varronem apud Cannas superavit. Cumque urbem capere posset, in Campaniam devertit, cuius deliciis elanguit. Et cum ad tertium ab urbe lapidem castra posuisset, tempestatibus repulsus primum a Fabio Maximo frustratus, deinde a Valerio Flacco repulsus, a Graccho et Marcello fugatus, in Africam revocatus, a Scipione superatus, ad Antiochum regem Syriae confugit eumque hostem Romanis fecit; quo victo ad Prusiam regem Bithyniae concessit; unde Romana legatione repetitus hausto, quod sub gemma anuli habebat, veneno absumptus est, positus apud Libyssam in arca lapidea, in qua hodieque inscriptum est: Hannibal hic situs est.

[1] novem annos *Pichl*.
[2] Cremeram *Vop* Trebeiam *C* Trebiam *NfRLS Pichl*.

XLII

HANNIBAL, son of Hamilcar, at the age of eleven was brought by his father before an altar, where he swore an oath of perpetual hatred against the Romans. After that, he was a companion and soldier in his father's camp. After his father's death, seeking a motive for war, he destroyed Saguntum, which was allied to the Romans, within six months. Then he opened the way in the Alps and crossed into Italy. He defeated Publius Scipio at the Ticinus River, Sempronius Longus at the Cremera River, Flaminius at Lake Trasimenus, and Paullus and Varro at Cannae. Although he could have taken Rome, he turned aside to Campania, by whose pleasures he was weakened. And when he had made camp three miles from Rome, storms drove him back. First of all he was frustrated by Fabius Maximus, then driven back by Valerius Flaccus, forced into flight by Gracchus and Marcellus, and recalled to Africa where he was defeated by Scipio. He fled to Antiochus, king of Syria, and made him an enemy of the Romans. After the defeat of Antiochus, Hannibal withdrew to Prusias, king of Bithynia. Demanded by a Roman legation, he drank poison, which he had concealed under the stone of his ring, and died. At Libyssa, he was placed in a stone coffin on which even today is the inscription: Here lies Hannibal.

XLIII
(49, 26)

Q<small>UINTUS</small> F<small>ABIUS</small> M<small>AXIMUS</small> C<small>UNCTATOR</small>, Verrucosus[1] a verruca in labris[2] ita, Ovicula a clementia morum, consul de Liguribus triumphavit. Hannibalem mora fregit. Minucium magistrum equitum imperio sibi aequari passus est; et[3] nihilo minus periclitanti subvenit. Hannibalem in agro Falerno inclusit. Marium Statilium transfugere ad hostes volentem equo et armis donatis retinuit, et Lucano cuidam fortissimo ob amorem mulieris infrequenti eandem emptam dono dedit. Tarentum ab hostibus recepit, Herculis signum inde translatum in Capitolio dedicavit. De redemptione captivorum cum hostibus pepigit; quod pactum cum a senatu improbaretur, fundum suum ducentis milibus vendidit et fidei satisfecit.

[1] ut verucosus *NfRLCS*
[2] labris sita *op Pichl.*
[3] et *om. op Pichl.*

XLIII

Quintus Fabius Maximus Cunctator, named Verrucosus (Warty) because of a wart on his lips, and Ovicula (Lambie) because of his mild disposition, celebrated as consul a triumph over the Ligurians. He broke Hannibal by his delaying tactics. He permitted Minucius, his master of the cavalry, to be given command equal to his own. Nevertheless, he aided Minucius when he was in danger. He confined Hannibal in Falernian country. By offering gifts of a horse and weapons, he restrained Marius Statilius, who wanted to defect to the enemy. Another individual, Lucan by name, a very brave person, was regularly absent from his standard because of his love for a woman. Fabius bought the woman and gave her as a gift to Lucan. He retook Tarentum from the enemy; he brought an image of Hercules from there and dedicated it in the Capitol. He made terms with the enemy for ransoming captives. When the agreement was not ratified by the Senate, he sold his own farm for 200,000 sesterces and honored his promise.

XLIV
(50, 12)

Publius Scipio Nasica, a senatu vir optimus iudicatus,
Matrem deum hospitio recepit. Adversum[1] auspicia cum
consulem se a Graccho nominatum comperisset, magistratu se abdicavit. Censor statuas, quas sibi quisque in
foro per ambitionem ponebat sustulit. Consul Delminium[2] urbem Dalmatarum expugnavit. Imperatoris nom-
en a militibus et a senatu triumphum oblatum recusavit.
Eloquentia primus, iuris scientia consultissimus, ingenio
sapientissimus fuit,[3] unde vulgo Corculum dictus.

[1] Is cum adversum auspicia *Sop Pichl.*
[2] Delminium *ƒ Pichl.* Delminum *NSopR* Delminii *V* Delmurum
C Delumium *L*
[3] fuit *om. op Pichl.*

XLIV

PUBLIUS SCIPIO NASICA, honored by the Senate with the title of vir optimus (best man), received the Mother of the gods with hospitality. Having learned that he had been named consul by Gracchus under unfavorable omens, he resigned his magistracy. As censor he removed the statues which ambitious people set up in their own honor in the Forum. As consul, he stormed Delminium, the city of the Dalmatians. He refused the title of imperator, which his soldiers extended to him, and a triumph, which the Senate offered. He was distinguished in eloquence, most skilled in knowledge of law, most prudent in nature, and because of this was commonly called Corculum (Goodheart).

XLV
(50, 22)

Marcus Marcellus Virdomarum[1] Gallorum ducem singulari proelio fudit. Spolia[2] opima Iovi Feretrio tertius a Romulo consecravit. Hannibalem posse apud Nolam locorum angustia adiutus vinci docuit. Syracusas per tres annos expugnavit. Et cum per calumniam triumphus a senatu negaretur, de sua sententia in Albano monte triumphavit. Quinquies consul insidiis Hannibalis deceptus et magnifice sepultus. Ossa Romam remissa a praedonibus intercepta perierunt.

[1] Virdomarum *scripsi* Viridomarum *op Pichl.* vir Romanus *VNfRLCS*

[2] Spolia opima Iovi Feretrio tertius a Romulo consecravit. Hannibalem posse apud Nolam locorum angustia adiutus vinci docuit *scripsi* Spolia opima Iovi Feretrio tertius a Romulo consecravit. Primus docuit, quomodo milites cederent nec terga praeberent. Hannibalem apud Nolam locorum angustia adiutus vinci docuit. *op Pichl.* opima . . . Nolam *om. cum lacuna V om. sine lacuna fRLCNS*

XLV

Marcus Marcellus vanquished Virdomarus, the leader of the Gauls, in individual combat. He was the third person after Romulus to consecrate the spoils of honor to Jupiter Feretrius. Aided by the narrowness of the region at Nola, he showed that Hannibal could be defeated. He besieged Syracuse for three years. When the Senate, through chicanery, refused to grant him a triumph, by his own decision he celebrated a triumph on the Alban mount. A consul five times, he was trapped in an ambush by Hannibal; he was given a magnificent burial. His bones were being returned to Rome but were lost when robbers intercepted them.

XLVI
(51, 3)

HANNIBALE Italiam devastante ex responso librorum
Sibylinorum Mater deum e Pessinunte[1] accersita cum adverso Tiberi veheretur, repente in alto stetit. Et cum
moveri nullis viribus posset, ex libris cognitum castissi-
mae demum feminae manu moveri posse. Tum Claudia
virgo Vestalis falso incesti suspecta deam oravit, ut, si
pudicam sciret, sequeretur, et zona imposita navem
movit. Simulacrum[2] Matris deum advexit. Templum
aedificatur Nasicae qui vir optimus iudicabatur.

[1] Pessinunte *NfRSp* Pessimunte *Vo* Pesimorite *L* a Pessimonte *C* a
Pessinunte *Pichl.*

[2] Simulacrum Matris deum tum templum aedificatur iudicabatur
quasi hospiti datum *op* Simulacrum Matris deum dum templum aedificatur, Nasicae, qui vir optimus iudicabatur, quasi hospiti datum
Pichl.

XLVI

WHEN HANNIBAL was devastating Italy, at the response of the Sibylline Books, the statue of the Mother of the gods was brought from Pessinus. When it was brought opposite the Tiber, it suddenly stopped in the sea. When no force could move the statue, it was learned from the books that it could be moved only by the hand of the most chaste woman. Then Claudia, a Vestal Virgin falsely suspected of incest, beseeched the goddess to follow her if she knew her to be virtuous. Claudia attached her girdle to the ship and moved it. She conveyed the statue of the Mother of the gods. Nasica, honored with the title of vir optimus, built a temple.

XLVII
(51, 13)

Marcus Porcius Cato, genere Tusculanus, a Valerio Flacco Romam sollicitatus, tribunus militum in Sicilia, quaestor sub Scipione fortissimus, praetor iustissimus fuit: in praetura Sardiniam subegit, ubi ab Ennio Graecis litteris institutus. Consul Celtiberos domuit et, ne rebellare possent, litteras ad singulas civitates misit, ut muros diruerent. Cum unaquaeque sibi soli imperari putaret, fecerunt. Syriaco bello tribunus militum sub Marco Acilio Glabrione occupatis Thermopylarum iugis praesidium hostium depulit. Censor Lucium Flaminium consularem senatu movit, quod ille in Gallia ad cuiusdam scorti spectaculum eiectum quendam e carcere in convivio iugulari iussisset. Basilicam suo nomine primus fecit. Matronis ornamenta erepta Oppia lege repetentibus restitit.[1] Accusator assiduus malorum Galbam octogenarius accusavit, ipse quadragies quater accusatus gloriose absolutus. Carthaginem delendam censuit. Post[2] octoginta annos filium genuit. Imago huius funeris gratis produci solet.

[1] restitit *Schott* restituit *omnes codd.*
[2] Post . . . genuit *om. NfRLC*

XLVII

MARCUS PORCIUS CATO, Tusculan by birth, urged to
Rome by Valerius Flaccus, served as military tribune in
Sicilia, a very brave quaestor under Scipio, and a very
just praetor. While praetor, he subdued Sardinia, where
he was instructed in Greek literature by Ennius. As consul, he overcame the Celtiberians and, to prevent rebellion, sent a letter instructing each state to destroy its
walls. Since each thought the order was given only to
them, they all complied. As a military tribune under M.
Acilius Glabrio in the Syrian War, he drove off a garrison
of the enemy from their occupied pass of Thermopylae.
As censor, he removed Lucius Flaminius, an ex-consul,
from the Senate because he had ordered that a certain
man be brought from prison and strangled at a banquet
as a show for some prostitute. He was the first to build a
basilica in his own name. He resisted attempts by the
women to reclaim their jewelry, which was seized by
reason of the Oppian Law. Constantly a plaintiff, even
at eighty, he accused Galba of evil. He himself was accused forty-four times and was acquitted gloriously. He
thought that Carthage ought to be destroyed. When he
was over eighty, a son was born to him. His statue is
usually carried in procession on the occasion of a funeral.

XLVIII
(52, 5)

HASDRUBAL, frater Hannibalis, ingentibus copiis in
Italiam traiecit, actumque[1] de Romano imperio erat, si
iungere[2] Hannibali potuisset. Sed Claudius Nero qui
in Apulia cum Hannibale castra coniunxerat relicta in
castris parte cum delectis ad Hasdrubalem properavit et
se Livio collegae apud Senam oppidum et Metaurum
flumen coniunxit amboque Hasdrubalem vicerunt. Nero
regressus pari celeritate, qua venerat, caput Hasdrubalis
ante vallum Hannibalis proiecit. Quo ille viso vinci se
fortuna Carthaginis confessus. Ob haec Livius triumphans, Nero ovans urbem introierunt.

[1]actumque erat *Pichl.*
[2] iungere se *p Pichl.*

XLVIII

HASDRUBAL, Hannibal's brother, crossed into Italy with vast supplies; it would have been the end of Roman command if he could have joined Hannibal. But Claudius Nero, who had made camp near Hannibal in Apulia, left part of his force in camp and hurried with a select body of troops to Hasdrubal. He joined his colleague Livius at the town of Sena on the Metaurus River, and both defeated Hasdrubal. Nero returned to camp as speedily as he had gone forth and cast the head of Hasdrubal before the fortification of Hannibal. When Hannibal saw it, he acknowledged that he had been defeated by the fortune of Carthage. On account of these things, Livius entered the city celebrating a triumph, Nero an ovation.

XLIX
(52, 17)

Publius Scipio ex virtutibus[1] nominatus Africanus, Iovis
filius creditus: nam antequam conciperetur, serpens in
lecto matris eius apparuit, et ipsi parvulo draco circum-
fusus nihil nocuit. In Capitolium intempesta nocte eun-
tem nunquam canes latraverunt. Nec hic quicquam prius
coepit, quam in cella Iovis diutissime sedisset quasi divi-
nam mentem accepisset.[2] Decem et octo annorum
patrem apud Ticinum[3] singulari virtute servavit. Clade
Cannensi nobilissimos iuvenes Italiam deserere cupientes
sua auctoritate compescuit. Reliquias incolumes per
media hostium castra Canusium perduxit. Viginti quattuor annorum praetor in Hispaniam missus Carthaginem, qua die venit, cepit. Virginem pulcherrimam, ad
cuius adspectum concurrebatur, ad se vetuit adduci
patrique eius sponsor astitit. Hasdrubalem Magonem-
que, fratres Hannibalis, Hispania expulit. Amicitiam
cum Syphace, Maurorum rege, coniunxit. Massinissam
in societatem[4] recepit. Victor domum regressus consul
ante annos factus concedente collega in Africam classem[5]
traicit. Hasdrubalis et Syphacis castra una nocte perrupit.
Revocatum ex Italia Hannibalem superavit. Victis Car-
thaginensibus[6] leges imposuit. Bello Antiochi legatus
fratri fuit; captum filium gratis recepit. A Petillio Ateio[7]
tribuno plebis repetundarum accusatus librum rationum
in conspectu populi scidit: "Hac die," inquit, "Carthaginem vici; quare, bonum factum, in Capitolium eamus et
diis supplicemus!" Inde in voluntarium exilium con-

110

XLIX

PUBLIUS SCIPIO, because of his military achievements, was given the name Africanus. He was believed to be a son of Jupiter, because a serpent appeared in his mother's bed before he was conceived, and when he was very little, a snake encircled but did not harm him. Dogs never barked at him as he went to the Capitol in the dead of night. Scipio never began anything before he had sat for the longest time in a shrine of Jupiter, as if to learn the divine plan. At eighteen, he saved his father at Ticinus by his extraordinary courage. At the slaughter of Cannae, he restrained by his own authority very noble young men who desired to abandon Italy. He led the remnants of the force unharmed to Canusium, through the midst of the enemy camp.

At the age of twenty-four, he was sent as a praetor to Spain; he took Carthage on the day of his arrival. He did not permit a very beautiful girl, whom people used to gather to see, to be brought to him, and he stood as surety for her father. He drove Hasdrubal and Mago, Hannibal's brothers, out of Spain. He made alliances with Syphax, king of the Moors, and Massinissa. Returning home as victor, he was made consul before reaching the required age. With the agreement of his colleague, he crossed a fleet into Africa. He broke through the camp of Hasdrubal and Syphax in one night. He defeated Hannibal, who had been recalled from Italy. He imposed laws on the conquered Cartha-

cessit, ubi reliquam egit aetatem. Moriens ab uxore petiit, ne corpus suum Romam referretur.

[1] virtutibus *VNLCS* a virtute *fRop* ex virtute Africanus dictus *Pichl.*

[2] acciperet *op Pichl.*

[3] apud Vaticanum *V*

[4] societatem *Lop Pichl.* societate *VfRCNS*

[5] classem *Nfop Pichl.* classe *VRLCS*

[6] Carthaginiensibus *Pichl.*

[7] Actaeo *f Pichl.*

ginians. He was a legate to his brother in the war with Antiochus; he received his captured son back from Antiochus without ransom. He was accused of extortion by Petillius Ateius, the plebian tribune; in view of the populace, he ripped his book of accounts and said: "On this day I conquered Carthage. A blessing has been gained. Let us therefore go to the Capitol and pray to the gods." Then he retired to voluntary exile for the rest of his life. While dying, he asked his wife not to return his body to Rome.

L
(53, 18)

Livius Salinator primo consul de Illyriis triumphavit, deinde ex invidia peculatus reus ab omnibus tribubus excepta Metia condemnatus. Iterum cum Claudio Nerone inimico suo consul, ne respublica discordia male administraretur, amicitiam cum eo iunxit et de Hasdrubale triumphavit. Censor cum eodem collega omnes tribus excepta Metia aerarias fecit, stipendio privavit eo crimine, quod aut prius se iniuste condemnassent aut postea tantos honores non recte tribuissent.

L

Lɪᴠɪᴜs Sᴀʟɪɴᴀᴛᴏʀ celebrated a triumph over the Illyrians in his first consulship; then, out of jealousy, he was accused of embezzlement and condemned by all the tribes, with the exception of the Metian tribe. In his second consulship, with his enemy Claudius Nero as a colleague, he made a friendly agreement with him so that the administration of the republic might function well; he celebrated a triumph over Hasdrubal. Censor with the same colleague, he taxed all the tribes, with the exception of the Metian. He deprived them of military pay, charging that they either had previously condemned him unjustly or had bestowed improperly such great honors on him afterward.

LI
(54, 3)

QUINTUS FLAMINIUS, Flaminii, qui apud Trasumenum periit, filius, consul Macedoniam sortitus, ducibus Charopae principis pastoribus provinciam ingressus regem Philippum proelio fudit, castris exuit. Filium eius Demetrium obsidem accepit, quem pecunia[1] mulctatum in regnum restituit. A Nabide[2] quoque[3] Lacedaemonio[4] filium obsidem accepit. Ludos Iunoni[5] Samiae per praeconem pronuntiavit. Legatus etiam ad Prusiam ut Hannibalem repeteret, missus.[6]

[1] quem pecunia . . . obsidem accepit *om. p*

[2] Nabide *C Pichl.* Anabidi *VNL* Nabidi *ƒRS* Anabi vel navidis *o*

[3] quoque *om. o*

[4] Lacedaemonio *NƒRLCS Pichl.* Lacedaemonii *V* Lacedaemoniis *o*

[5] Iunonis *op Pichl.*

[6] missus. Idem postea proconsul Phillipum bellum renovantem et cum eo Trachas Macedonas Illyrios multasque gentes partium ipsius bello subegit *op*

LI

QUINTUS FLAMINIUS, son of the Flaminius who died at Lake Trasimenus, obtained Macedonia by lot as consul. Guided by shepherds of the sovereign Charopa, he entered the province, routed King Phillip in battle, and drove him from his camp. He received Phillip's son Demetrius as hostage; he restored Phillip to the throne after punishing him with a fine. He received also as hostage the son of Nabis of Sparta. He proclaimed the games to Juno at Samia through a herald. He was a legate sent to Prusias to bring back Hannibal.

LII
(54, 12)

Q<small>UINTUS</small> F<small>ULVIUS</small> N<small>OBILIOR</small> consul Vettonas[1] Oretanos-
que[2] superavit, unde ovans urbem introiit. Consul[3]
Aetolos qui bello Macedonico interfuerant, post ad Antiochum defecerant, proeliis frequentibus victos et in Am-
braciam oppidum coactos in deditionem accepit, tamen
signis tabulisque pictis spoliavit; de quibus triumphavit.
Quam victoriam per se magnificam M.[4] Ennius amicus
eius insigni laude celebravit.

[1] Vettonas *Schott Pichl.* ettonas *Vop* etholas *NƒRLCS*
[2] Oretanos *NƒLCS* Orecanos *V* Suritanos *op*
[3] Consul Aetolos qui bello Macedonico Romanis affuerant *op*
Pichl. Conateos qui bello Macedonico interfuerant *VƒRLCNS*
[4] M. Ennius *ƒLS* Meim' *V* Ennius *op Pichl.* M. eni *R* M. Emin' *C*
Quintus Marcus Ennius *N*

LII

Quintus Fulvius Nobilior, having, as consul, defeated
the Vettones and the Oretanians, entered the city celebrating a triumph. Still in his consulship, he frequently
defeated in battle the Aetolians, who had taken part in
the Macedonian War and later had deserted to Antiochus. He drove them to the town of Ambracia where he
accepted their surrender (but he still plundered their
statues and paintings), for which he celebrated a triumph. His friend Ennius celebrated with remarkable
praise this victory, so magnificent in itself.

LIII
(54, 20)

Scipio Asiaticus, frater Africani, infirmo corpore, tamen in Africa virtutis nomine a fratre laudatus, consul Antiochum regem Syriae legato fratre apud Sipylum montem, cum arcus hostium pluvia hebetati fuissent, vicit et regni relicti[1] parte privavit: hinc Asiaticus dictus. Post reus pecuniae interceptae, ne in carcerem duceretur, Gracchus pater tribunus plebis intercessit.[2] Marcus Cato censor equum ei ignominiae causa ademit.

[1] relicti parte *NfRLC* relicti a patre *V* relicta a patre *S* parte *op Pichl.*

[2] inimicus eius intercessit *op Pichl.*

LIII

SCIPIO ASIATICUS, brother of Africanus, although of weak body, was nevertheless praised by his brother for his courage in Africa. As consul, and with his brother as lieutenant, he defeated Antiochus, king of Syria, at Mount Sipylus, when rain damaged the bows of the enemy; and he deprived Antiochus of part of the kingdom he had inherited. Because of this he was given the name Asiaticus. Later, he was accused of stealing money, and Gracchus, his father, the plebian tribune, interceded so that he might not be taken to prison. To disgrace Scipio, the censor Marcus Cato took away his horse.

LIV
(55, 6)

ANTIOCHUS, rex Syriae, nimia opum fiducia bellum Romanis intulit, specie Lysimachiae repetundae, quam a maioribus suis in Thracia quondam[1] Romani possidebant, statimque Graeciam[2] insulasque eius occupavit. In Euboea luxuria elanguit. Adventu Acilii[3] Glabrionis excitus[4] Thermopylas occupavit, unde industria Marci Catonis eiectus in Asiam refugit. Navali proelio, cui Hannibalem praefecerat, a Lucio Aemilio Regillo superatus filium Scipionis Africani, quem inter navigandum ceperat, patri remisit, qui ei quasi pro reddenda gratia suasit, ut amicitiam Romanam peteret. Antiochus spreto consilio apud Sipylum[5] montem cum Lucio Scipione conflixit. Victus et ultra Taurum montem relegatus, a sodalibus, quos temulentus in convivio pulsaverat,[6] occisus est.

[1] conditam Romani *Pichl.*
[2] Graeciam *Sop Pichl.* regiam *VNƒRLC*
[3] Acilii *NƒRLCS* arciaci *V* acivi *op* M. Acilii *Pichl.*
[4] excitatus *op Pichl.*
[5] Sipylum *RLCSop Pichl.* Sapilum *VN*
[6] pulsarat *op Pichl.*

LIV

Antiochus, king of Syria, too confident of his strength, waged war with the Romans on the pretext of recovering Lysimachia, which the Romans formerly received as possession from his ancestors in Thracia. Antiochus at once occupied Greece and its islands. In Euboea, he became languid from luxury. Aroused by the arrival of Acilius Glabrio, he seized Thermopylae. He was driven out of there by the industriousness of Marcus Cato, and he sought refuge in Asia. He was defeated by Lucius Aemilius Regillus in a naval battle in which he had appointed Hannibal as leader. Antiochus had captured the son of Scipio Africanus during the sailing, and he returned him to his father, who, as if to return the favor, tried to persuade him to seek the friendship of Rome. Antiochus rejected his advice and met Lucius Scipio in battle at Mount Sipylus. He was defeated and banished beyond Mount Taurus. He was killed by companions whom he had drunkenly struck at a banquet.

LV
(55, 21)

Gaius[1] Manlius Vulso missus ad ordinandam Scipionis Asiatici provinciam cupidine triumphi bellum Pisidis et Gallograecis, qui Antiocho affuerant, intulit. His facile victis inter captivos uxor regis Orgiaguntis[2] centurioni cuidam in custodiam data; a quo vi stuprata de iniuria tacuit et post impetrata redemptione marito adulterum interficiendum tradidit.

[1] Gaius Manlius *Pichl.* Gneus Manlius *NʄRLCS* Gaius Manilius *Vop*
[2] Orgiaguntis *VNʄRL* Orgiagantis *C* Orgiagontis *Sop Pichl.*

LV

Gaius Manlius Vulso was sent to set in order the province of Scipio Asiaticus. His desire to celebrate a triumph led him to wage war on the Pisidians and the Galatians who had helped Antiochus. They were easily defeated; the wife of King Orgiaguns was among the captives. She was put in the custody of a certain centurion who raped her. She remained quiet about the injury and, after ransom was obtained, handed the adulterer over to her husband to be killed.

LVI
(56, 1)

Lucius Aemilius Paullus, filius eius, qui apud Cannas
cecidit, primo consulatu, quem post tres repulsas adeptus
erat, de Liguribus triumphavit. Rerum gestarum ordinem in tabula pictum publice posuit. Iterum consul Persen Philippi filium regem Macedonum apud Samothracas[1] cepit; quem vinctum[2] flevit et assidere sibi iussit,
tamen in triumphum duxit. In hac laetitia duos filios
amisit et progressus ad populum gratias fortunae egit,
quod, si quid adversi reipublicae imminebat, sua esset
calamitate decisum. Ob haec omnia ei a populo et senatu[3]
concessum est, ut ludis circensibus triumphali veste uteretur. Ob huius licentiam[4] et paupertatem post mortem
eius dos uxori nisi venditis possessionibus non potuit
exsolvi.

[1] Samothracas deos *op*
[2] vinctum *VN* victum *fLCSop Pichl.*
[3] a senatu *Cop*
[4] licentiam *VNfRLC* letitiam et licentiam *S* continentiam *op Pichl.*

LVI

Lucius Aemilius Paullus, son of the man who died at Cannae, in his first consulship, which he had obtained after three rejections, celebrated a triumph over the Ligurians. He set up at public expense a painting depicting his accomplishments. In his second consulship, he captured the Macedonian king, Perses, the son of Phillip, at Samothrace. He wept over Perses' confinement and ordered that Perses stay by his side; nevertheless he included him in his triumph. In the midst of this rejoicing, he lost two sons. He went before the people and gave thanks to fortune because whatever adversity had threatened the state had been ended by his own calamity. On account of all these things, the people and Senate granted him the privilege of enjoying the circus games in triumphal garb. Because of his licentiousness and his poverty, only the sale of his possessions could repay the dowry to his wife after his death.

LVII
(56, 16)

Tiberius Sempronius Gracchus nobilissima familia
ortus Scipionem Asiaticum quamvis inimicum duci in
carcerem non passus.[1] Praetor Galliam domuit, consul
Hispaniam, altero consulatu Sardiniam, tantumque captivorum adduxit, ut longa venditione res in proverbium
veniret "Sardi venales." Censor libertinos, qui rusticas
tribus occupaverant,[2] in quattuor urbanas divisit; ob
quod a populo collega eius Claudius (nam ipsum auc-
toritas tuebatur) reus factus; et cum eum duae classes
condemnassent, Tiberius iuravit se cum illo in exilium
iturum: ita reus absolutus.[3] Et[4] cum in domo Tiberii
duos[5] angues e geniali toro repsissent,[6] responso dato
eum de dominis periturum cuius sexus anguis fuisset
occisus, amore Corneliae coniugis marem iussit interfici.

[1] est passus *op Pichl.*
[2] occupaverant *VNCS* occuparant *fRLop Pichl.*
[3] absolutus est *Pichl.*
[4] Et *om Pichl.*
[5] duos *VfRCS* duo *NLop Pichl.*
[6] erepsissent *op Pichl.*

LVII

TIBERIUS SEMPRONIUS GRACCHUS, born of a very noble family, did not allow the imprisoning of Scipio Asiaticus, although he was a personal enemy. In his praetorship, he conquered Gaul; in his consulship, Spain; and in his second consulship, Sardinia. He brought so many captives that the lengthy sale gave rise to the saying, "Sardinians for sale." In his censorship, he divided the sons of freedmen, who had occupied rustic tribes, into four urban tribes. Because of this, the people made accusations against his colleague Claudius (for Tiberius was protected by his authority). When two classes had condemned him, Tiberius made an oath to go into exile with him; and so he was acquitted. When two snakes had crawled out from the marriage bed in Tiberius' home, the oracle responded that the first of the two masters of the house to die would be the one whose sex corresponded to the sex of the snake to be killed. Because of his love for his wife Cornelia, Tiberius ordered the male snake to be killed.

LVIII
(57, 3)

Publius Scipio Aemilianus, Paulli Macedonici filius, a Scipione Africano adoptatus, in Macedonia cum patre agens victum Persen tam pertinaciter persecutus est, ut media nocte in castra redierit. Lucullo in Hispania legatus apud Intercatiam oppidum provocatorem singulari proelio vicit. Muros hostiles[1] civitatis primus ascendit. Tribunus in Africa sub Tito Mallio[2] imperatore octo cohortes obsidione vallatas consilio et virtute servavit, a quibus corona obsidionali aurea donatus. Cum aedilitatem peteret, consul ante annos ultro factus Carthaginem intra sex menses delevit. Numantiam in Hispania correcta prius militum disciplina fame vicit: hic[3] Numantinus. Gaio[4] Laelio plurimum usus; ad reges adeundos missus duos secum praeter eum servos duxit. Ob res gestas superbus Gracchum iure caesum videri respondit; obstrepente populo: "Taceant," inquit, "quibus Italia noverca, non mater est;" et addidit: "Quos ego sub corona vendidi." Censor Mummio collega segniore in senatu ait: "Utinam mihi collegam aut dedissetis aut non dedissetis." Suscepta agrariorum causa domi repente exanimis inventus obvoluto capite elatus, ne livor in ore appareret. Huius patrimonium tam exiguum ut triginta duas libras argenti, duas et semilibram auri reliquerit.

---

[1] hostilis *op Pichl*.
[2] Mallio *VNRop* Manlio *ƒLS* Maulio *C* Manilio *Pichl*.

LVIII

PUBLIUS SCIPIO AEMILIANUS, son of Paullus Macedonicus, was adopted by Scipio Africanus. With his father and the army in Macedonia, he pursued the defeated Perses so tenaciously that he returned to camp in the middle of the night. As a legate to Lucullus in Spain, he defeated a challenger in single combat at the town Intercatia. He was the first to climb the walls of the enemy state. Tribune in Africa under the command of Titus Mallius, he saved, by his prudence and courage, eight cohorts which were surrounded by a blockade. The cohorts presented him with a golden siege crown.

Although he was campaigning for the aedileship, he was elected consul without seeking the office and before he had reached the required age. He destroyed Carthage within six months. He first restored the discipline of the troops and then conquered Numantia in Spain by depriving them of food; he was given the name Numantinus. He was an intimate friend of Gaius Laelius; sent to meet kings, he took two servants and Laelius with him. Elated by pride because of his exploits, he said that Gracchus' murder seemed just to him. When the populace cried out in opposition, he said, "Let them be quiet for whom Italia is a stepmother, not a mother," and he added, "Those whom I have sold as slaves." As censor with a rather inactive colleague, Mummius, he said in the Senate: "I wish either you had given me a colleague

[3] hic *VNop* hinc *ƒRLCS Pichl.*

[4] Gaio Laelio *Pichl.* Caelio Laelio *NƒLCS corrupt.* *V* Panetio philosopho *op* Laelio Laelio *R*

or you had not." After the cause of the partisans of the agrarian laws was undertaken, he was found dead suddenly at home; he was carried out with his head covered so that the bluish color on his face would not be seen. His estate was so small that he left only thirty-two pounds of silver and two and one-half of gold.

LIX
(57, 27)

Aᴜʟᴜs Hᴏsᴛɪʟɪᴜs Mᴀɴᴄɪɴᴜs praetor adversum Numantinos vetantibus avibus et nescio qua voce revocante profectus, cum ad Numantiam venisset, exercitum Pompei acceptum prius corrigere decrevit et solitudinem petiit. Eo die Numantini[1] forte sollemni nuptum filias locabant; et unam speciosam duobus competentibus pater puellae condicionem tulit, ut ei illa nuberet, qui hostis dexteram attulisset. Profecti iuvenes abscessum Romanorum in modum fugae properantium cognoscunt, et ad[2] suos referunt. Illi statim quattuor milibus suorum viginti milia Romanorum ceciderunt. Mancinus auctore Tiberio Graccho quaestore[3] in leges hostium foedus percussit; quo per senatum improbato Mancinus Numantinis deditus nec receptus, augurio in castra deductus, praeturam postea consecutus est.

[1] Numantinis *f Pichl*.

[2] rem ad suos *Pichl*.

[3] quaestore suo in leges hostium *op Pichl*. quaestore intelleges hostium *V*

LIX

Aulus Hostilius Mancinus, as praetor, set out against the Numantines in spite of opposing omens and some voice which called him back. On his arrival at Numantia, having received the army of Pompey, he decided first to reform it and sought a desert place. By chance, on that day the Numantines in their customary manner were giving their daughters in marriage. The father of one beautiful girl who was sought by two men promised that she would marry the one who brought back the right hand of an enemy. Setting out, the youths learned of the departure of the Romans, who hurried as if in flight, and they reported this to their countrymen. They, with four thousand of their own troops, at once killed twenty thousand Romans. Mancinus, counseled by the quaestor Tiberius Gracchus, struck a treaty according to the terms of the enemy. The Senate rejected it; Mancinus was surrendered to the Numantines but they refused to accept him. He was brought to camp because of augury, and he later obtained the praetorship.

LX
(58, 12)

Lucius Mummius, deleta[1] Achaia, Achaicus, adversum
Corinthios missus victoriam alieno labore quaesitam intercepit. Nam cum illos Metellus Macedonicus apud
Heracleam fudisset et duce Critolao privasset, cum lic-
toribus et paucis equitibus in Metelli claustra[2] properavit
et Corinthios apud Leucopetram vicit duce Diaeo,[3] qui
domum refugit eamque incendit. Coniugem[4] interfecit
et in ignem praecipitavit, ipse veneno interiit. Mummius[5]
Corinthum signis tabulisque spoliavit; quibus cum totam
replesset Italiam, in domum suam nihil contulit.

[1] devicta Achaia Achaicus dictus consul *op Pichl.*
[2] claustra *VNRS* castra *ʃLCop Pichl.*
[3] Diaeo *Pichl.* Dineo *omnes codd.*
[4] Coniugem interfecit *op Pichl. om. VNʃRLCS*
[5] Mummius *ʃo Pichl.* Munmius *V* Nummius *Lp* Muntius *C* Mam-
mius *N* Mumius *RS*

LX

Lucius Mummius, named Achaicus from the destruction of Achaia, having been sent against the Corinthians, took for himself the victory which was gained by the efforts of another. For when Metellus Macedonicus had routed them at Heraclea and had killed their leader Critolaus, Mummius hurried with his lictors and a few horsemen to the fortress of Metellus. At Leucopetra he defeated the Corinthians led by Dineus, who fled home and set it on fire. He killed his wife and hurled her body into the fire; he himself died by poison. Mummius plundered Corinth of statues and paintings, and although he filled all Italy with them, he brought nothing into his own home.

LXI
(58, 23)

Quintus Caecilius[1] Metellus, a[2] domita Macedonia Macedonicus,[3] praetor Pseudophilippum, qui idem Andriscus dictus est, vicit.[4] Invisus plebi ob nimiam severitatem et ideo post duas repulsas consul aegre factus Arbacos in Hispania domuit. Apud Contrebiam[5] oppidum cohortes loco pulsas redire et locum recipere iussit. Cum omnia proprio et subito consilio ageret, amico cuidam, quid acturus esset, roganti: "Tunicam," inquit, "meam exurerem, si eam consilium meum scire existimarem." Hic quattuor filiorum pater supremo tempore humeris eorum ad sepulcrum latus est; ex quibus tres consulares, unum etiam triumphantem vidit.

[1] Caecilius Metellus *Vop* Metellus Caecilius *NfRLCS*

[2] a *om. op Pichl.*

[3] Macedonicus dictus *op Pichl.*

[4] . . . vicit. Achaeos bis proelio fudit triumphandos Mummio tradidit. Invisus . . . *op Pichl.*

[5] Contrebiam *Colinaeus Pichl.* Cotebriam *VfR* Cantebriam *L* Cotrebiam *C* Cotebiam *NS* Cantabriam *op*

LXI

Quintus Caecilius Metellus, named Macedonicus from his conquest of Macedonia, as praetor defeated Pseudophilippus, who was also called Andriscus. Hated by the people because of his extreme severity (he was barely elected consul after two defeats), he conquered the Arbaci in Spain. At Contrebia, he ordered the cohorts who had been driven from the place to return and recapture their position. When he was directing operations in a peculiar and unexpected fashion, he answered thus a certain friend who had asked him what he was about to do: "I would burn my tunic if I thought that it knew my plan." He was the father of four sons and at his death was carried to his grave on their shoulders. He saw three of the sons become consuls and one even celebrate a triumph.

LXII
(59, 8)

QUINTUS CAECILIUS METELLUS NUMIDICUS, qui de Iugurtha rege triumphavit, censor Quintium, qui se Tiberii Gracchi filium mentiebatur, in censum non recepit. Idem in legem Apuleiam per vim latam iurare noluit,[1] quare in exilium actus Smyrnae exulavit. Calidia[2] deinde rogatione revocatus cum ludis forte litteras in theatro accepisset, non prius eas legere dignatus est, quam spectaculum finiretur. Metellae[3] sororis suae virum laudare noluit, quod is solus[4] iudicium contra leges detrectaverat.

[1] voluit *Vo*
[2] Calidia *Schott Pichl.* Claudia *omnes codd.*
[3] Metellae *Olivarius Pichl.* Metellum *omnes codd.*
[4] solus *Schott* solum *VfRLCNS* olim *op Pichl.*

LXII

Quintus Caecilius Metellus Numidicus, who celebrated a triumph over King Jugurtha, as censor did not record in the census Quintus, who was pretending to be the son of Tiberius Gracchus. Numidicus also refused to swear to observe the Apuleian Law which had been passed by force. For this reason, he was driven into exile, which he spent at Smyrna. He was later recalled by the Calidian decree. One day, a letter was delivered to him when he was present at the games in the theater; he did not think it proper to read it before the spectacle should finish. He did not want to praise his sister Metella's husband, because he alone had disapproved of a court decision against the laws.

LXIII
(59, 18)

Q‌uintus M‌etellus P‌ius, Numidici filius[1] patrem lacrimis et precibus assidue revocavit. Praetor bello sociali Quintum Popedium Marsorum ducem interfecit. Consul in Hispania Herculeios fratres oppressit, Sertorium Hispania expulit. Adolescens in petitione praeturae et pontificatus consularibus viris praelatus est.

[1] filius patrem *scripsi* filium *VNRL* filius Pius dictus quia patrem *op* filius Pius quia patrem *Pichl.* filius *ʄCS*

142

LXIII

QUINTUS METELLUS PIUS, the son of Numidicus, con-
tinuously sought his father's recall with tears and prayers. As praetor in the Social War, he killed Quintus
Popedius, the leader of the Marsi. While consul in Spain,
he subdued the Hirtuleii brothers and drove Sertorius
out of Spain. As a young man, he was granted preference
over men of consular rank in his candidacy for the
praetorship and the office of pontifex maximus.

LXIV
(59, 25)

Tiberius Gracchus, Africani ex filia nepos, quaestor Mancino in Hispania foedus eius flagitiosum probavit. Periculum deditionis eloquentiae gratia fugit.[1] Tribunus plebis legem tulit, ne quis plus mille agri iugera haberet. Octavio collega[2] intercedente novo exemplo magistratum abrogavit. Dein tulit, ut ex[3] ea pecunia, quae de[4] Attali hereditate erat, ageretur et populo divideretur. Deinde cum prorogare sibi potestatem vellet, adversis auspiciis in publicum processit statimque Capitolium petiit manum ad caput referens, quo salutem suam populo commendabat. Hoc nobilitas ita accepit, quasi diadema posceretur; segniterque cessante Mucio consule Scipio Nasica sequi se iussit, qui salvam rempublicam vellent, Gracchum in Capitolium persecutus oppressit. Cuius corpus Lucretii aedilis manu in Tiberim missum; unde ille Vispillo[5] dictus. Nasica ut invidiae subtraheretur, per speciem legationis in Asiam ablegatus est.

[1] effugit *Pichl*.

[2] collega intercedente *VNfLS* collegae intercedente *RC* collegae interdicenti *op* collegae intercedenti *Pichl*.

[3] de ea *Pichl*.

[4] ex Attali *Pichl*.

[5] Vispillo *VN* Vispilio *fRLCSop*

LXIV

Tɪʙᴇʀɪᴜs Gʀᴀᴄᴄʜᴜs, grandson of Scipio Africanus by his mother, as quaestor to Mancinus in Spain, approved his disgraceful treaty. His eloquence saved him from the danger of being surrendered to the enemy. As a plebian tribune, he passed a law prohibiting any person from owning more than one thousand acres of land. His colleague Octavius protested; in an unprecedented manner, Tiberius deprived him of his magistracy. Then he passed a bill so that the money from the inheritance of Attalus would be attended to and divided among the people. Wishing to prolong his power, he proceeded into the public assembly, although the omens were unfavorable, and immediately sought the Capitol; he raised his hand to his head as a sign that he was entrusting his safety to the people. The nobility interpreted this as a demand for a crown. While the consul Mucius lingered tardily, Scipio Nasica ordered all who wanted the republic safe to follow him. He pursued Gracchus to the Capitol and killed him. The aedile Lucretius threw Gracchus' body into the Tiber and because of this received the name Vispillo. Nasica was sent to Asia under pretext of an embassy in order to avoid the ill will of the people.

LXV
(60, 16)

GAIUS GRACCHUS pestilentem Sardiniam quaestor sortitus non veniente successore sua sponte discessit. Ascu-
lanae et Fregellanae[1] defectionis invidiam sustinuit.
Tribunus plebis agrarias et frumentarias leges tulit,
colonos etiam Capuam et Tarentum mittendos censuit.
Triumviros agris dividendis se et Fulvium Flaccum et
Gaium Crassum constituit. Minucio Rufo[2] tribuno
plebis legibus suis abrogante[3] in Capitolium venit;
ubi cum Antyllius[4] praeco Opimii consulis in turba
fuisset occisus, in forum descendit et imprudens contionem a tribuno plebis avocavit: qua re accersitus[5]
cum in senatum non venisset, armata familia Aventinum occupavit; ubi ab Opimio victus, dum a
templo Lunae desiluit,[6] talum intorsit et Pomponio[7]
amico apud portam Trigeminam, Publio Laetorio in
ponte Sublicio persequentibus resistente in locum[8]
Furinae[9] pervenit. Ibi vel sua vel servi Euphori manu
interfectus; caput a Septimuleio[10] amico Gracchi ad
Opimium relatum auro expensum fertur, propter avari-
tiam infuso plumbo gravius effectum.

[1] Fregellanae *V Pichl.* Fregalane *ƒL* Fregeliane *N* Fragellanae *CS*
Fregedanae *op*
[2] Rufo *op Pichl.* Ruco *VƒRLNCS*
[3] obrogante *ƒop Pichl.*
[4] Antullius *VƒLN* Amtullius *o* Anicullius *p* Antulius *RCS*
[5] arcessitus *op Pichl.*
[6] desiluit *scripsi* desilit *Pichl.* desiliit *omnes codd.*
[7] Pomponio *ƒC Pichl.* Pontino *VNRLCSop*
[8] locum *omnes codd.* lucum *Pichl.*
[9] Furinae *Machaneus* Furrianae *Vop* Furianae *NRLCS* Furranae *ƒ*
[10] Septimuleio *Pichl.* Septimio Atello *omnes codd.*

LXV

Gaius Gracchus, as quaestor, having received by lot a pestilential Sardinia, departed of his own accord before his successor had arrived. He endured the unpopularity from the rebellion of Asculum and Fregellae. As plebian tribune, he brought about the passage of the agrarian and grain laws; he even recommended that colonists should be sent to Capua and Tarentum. He established a three-man board consisting of himself, Fulvius Flaccus, and Gaius Crassus to divide the lands. When Minucius Rufus, a plebian tribune, opposed his laws, Gracchus came to the Capitol. When Antyllius, a herald of the consul Opimius, had been killed in the tumult, Gracchus descended to the Forum and imprudently called the assembly away from the tribune of the people. Summoned before the Senate for this, he did not come but seized the Aventine with his armed household. He was defeated by Opimius and, while leaping down from the temple of the Moon, twisted his ankle. While those following him were opposed by his friend Pomponius at the Trigemina Gate and Publius Laetorius at the wooden bridge, he reached the place of Furina. There he either killed himself or was killed by his slave, Euphorus. His friend Septimuleius is said to have carried Gracchus' head to Opimius and sold it for its weight in gold after greedily having put lead inside to increase the weight.

LXVI
(61, 13)

Marcus Livius Drusus, genere et eloquentia magnus, sed ambitiosus et superbus, aedilis munus magnificentissimum dedit. Ubi Remmio collegae quaedam de utilitate rei publicae suggerenti: "Quid tibi," inquit, "cum republica nostra?" Quaestor in Asia nullis insignibus uti voluit, ne quid ipso esset insignius. Tribunus plebis Latinis civitatem, plebi agros, equitibus curiam, senatui iudicia permisit. Nimiae liberalitatis fuit: ipse etiam professus nemini se ad largiendum praeter caelum et caenum reliquisse; ideoque cum pecunia egeret, multa contra dignitatem fecit. Magudulsam Mauritaniae principem ob regis simultatem profugum accepta pecunia Boccho prodidit, quem ille elephanto obiecit. Adherbalem filium regis Numidarum obsidem domi suae suppressit redemptionem eius occulte[1] a patre sperans. Caepionem inimicum actionibus suis resistentem ait se de saxo Tarpeio praecipitaturum. Consuli[2] legibus agrariis resistenti ita collum in comitio obtorsit, ut multus sanguis efflueret e naribus; quem illa luxuria opprobrans muriam[3] de turdis esse dicebat. Deinde ex gratia[4] in invidiam venit. Nam plebs acceptis agris gaudebat, expulsi dolebant, equites in senatum lecti laetabantur;[5] senatus permissis iudiciis exultabat, sed societatem cum equitibus aegre ferebat. Unde Livius anxius, ut Latinorum postulata differret, qui promissam civitatem flagitabant, repente in publico concidit sive morbo comitiali seu hausto caprino sanguine, semianimis domum relatus.

LXVI

Marcus Livius Drusus, distinguished in birth and eloquence, but ambitious and proud, put on a very costly public show as aedile. When his colleague Remmius was advocating certain measures useful for the republic, Drusus said to him: "What do you have to do with our republic?" As quaestor in Asia, he did not want to use any marks of distinction, lest anything be more outstanding than he. As plebian tribune, he opened citizenship to the Latins, public lands to the plebs, the Senate House to the Knights and the right of jury to the Senate. He was too liberal; he himself even declared publicly that he had left nothing for anyone to bestow except sky and filth. And thus, when he needed money, he did many things unworthy of his office.

Magudulsa, a prince of Mauritania, was a fugitive because of the king's hatred. Drusus received money for delivering him to Bocchus, who threw Magudulsa into the path of an elephant. He kept Adherbal, son of the Numidian king, prisoner in his own home and hoped for a secret ransom from the father. Caepio, an enemy, was opposing his motions; Drusus threatened to hurl him from the Tarpeian Rock. So violently did he twist the neck of the consul who was opposing his agrarian laws in the comitium that blood flowed profusely from his nose; reproaching him for that luxurious way of life, he said that the blood was brine from a flatfish. Drusus' popularity afterwards declined, and he became hated.

Vota pro illo per Italiam publice suscepta sunt. Et cum Latini consulem in Albano[6] interfecturi essent, Philippum admonuit, ut caveret; unde in senatu accusatus, cum domum se reciperet, immisso inter turbam percussore corruit. Invidia caedis apud Philippum et Caepionem fuit.

[1] occultam *op Pichl.*

[2] Philippo consuli *op Pichl.*

[3] muriam de turdis esse dicebat. *op Pichl.* mori aut detur dixisse dicebat *fL* mori autem detur dixisse *NS* disesse *V* dixisse *R* duxisse *C*

[4] gratia nimia *op Pichl.*

[5] laetabantur, sed praeteriti querebantur *op Pichl.*

[6] albano monte *CSp Pichl.*

For although the plebs obtaining land rejoiced, the ones driven off grieved. The Knights who were elected for the Senate were happy, and the Senate was greatly pleased with receiving the right of jury, but it resented the association with the Knights. Because of this, Livius was anxious to postpone the demands of the Latins, who were pressing for their promised citizenship. He suddenly collapsed in public, either from epilepsy or because he had drunk goat's blood, and was carried home half-dead. Public prayers were offered for him throughout Italy. When the Latins were going to kill the consul Philip on the Alban Mountain, Drusus warned him to be on his guard. Because of this, he was accused in the Senate and, when he was returning home, was killed by an assassin dispatched in the midst of the crowd. The hatred arising from his murder fell upon Philip and Caepio.

LXVII
(62, 21)

Gaius Marius, septies consul, Arpinas, humili loco natus, primis honoribus per ordinem functus, legatus Metello in Numidia criminando[1] consulatum adeptus Iugurtham captum ante currum egit. In proximum annum consul ultro factus Cimbros in Gallia apud Aquas Sextias, Teutonas in Italia in campo Savidio[2] vicit deque his triumphavit. Usque sextum consulatum per ordinem factus Apuleium tribunum plebi[3] et Glauciam[4] praetorem seditiosos ex senatus consulto interemit. Et cum Sulpicia rogatione provinciam Syllae eriperet, armis ab eo victus Minturnis in palude latuit.[5] Inventus et in carcerem coniectus immissum percussorem Gallum vultus auctoritate deterruit acceptaque navicula in Africam traiecit, ubi diu exulavit. Mox Cinnana dominatione revocatus ruptis ergastulis exercitum fecit caesisque inimicis iniuriam ultus septimo consulatu, ut quidam ferunt, voluntaria morte decessit.

[1] criminando eum *op Pichl.*
[2] Savidio *fCS* Saviclio *V* Sanido *L* Sanidio *S* Sanicho *N* Raudio *op Pichl.*
[3] plebi *Vop* plebis *NfLCS Pichl.*
[4] Glauciam *Lop Pichl.* Clautiam *VNfRCS*
[5] delituit *op Pichl.*

LXVII

Gaius Marius, who was consul seven times, was born in humble circumstances at Arpinum and discharged the duties of the highest offices in order. He became a lieutenant to Metellus in Numidia and obtained the consulship by making accusations. He captured Jugurtha and drove him before his chariot in his triumph. In the next year, when he was made consul without seeking the office, he conquered the Cimbri in Gaul at Aquae Sextiae and the Teutones in Italy in the Raudian Plain, and because of his victories over these peoples he celebrated a triumph. In his sixth successive consulship, supported by a "senatus consultum" he killed the seditious Apuleius and Glaucia, the former a plebian tribune and the latter a praetor. At the time when the Sulpician Bill provided that he should take over Sulla's province, he was defeated in battle by Sulla and so concealed himself in the swamp of Minturnae. Found and imprisoned, he terrified the Gallic assassin sent in against him by the forcefulness of his facial expression. He obtained a boat and crossed to Africa, where he remained in exile for a long time. Afterwards, when he was recalled in the tyranny of Cinna, he made up an army by breaking open the prisons and avenged his injury by slaughtering his enemies. In his seventh consulship, as some say, he committed suicide.

LXVIII
(63, 9)

GAIUS MARIUS filius viginti septem annorum consulatum invasit, quem honorem tam immaturum mater flevit. Hic patri saevitia similis curiam armatus obsedit, inimicos trucidavit, quorum corpora in Tiberim praecipitavit. In apparatu belli, quod contra Syllam parabatur, apud Sacriportum vigiliis et labore defessus sub divo requievit et absens victus fugae, non pugnae interfuit. Praeneste confugit, ubi per Lucretium Afellam obsessus temptata per cuniculum fuga, cum omnia saepta intelligeret, iugulandum se Pontio Telesino praebuit.

LXVIII

GAIUS MARIUS, son of Marius, seized the consulship at
the age of twenty-seven. His mother wept at such a premature public office. Marius, as cruel as his father, armed,
besieged the Senate House, slaughtered his enemies, and
hurled their bodies into the Tiber. While preparing for
war against Sulla, he rested in the open air at Sacriportus,
exhausted from sleeplessness and work. During his absence, he was defeated; and he shared in the flight, not
the battle. He took refuge in Praeneste, where he was
besieged by Lucretius Afella. He attempted to flee by a
passage under ground, but when he learned that every-
thing was guarded, he offered himself to Pontius Telesinus to be killed.

LXIX
(63, 20)

Lucius Cornelius Cinna flagitiosissimus rempublicam summa crudelitate vastavit. Primo consulatu legem de exulibus revocandis ferens ab Octavio collega prohibitus et honore privatus urbe profugit vocatisque ad pilleum servis adversarios vicit. Octavium interfecit, Ianiculum occupavit. Iterum et tertio consulem se ipse fecit. Quarto consulatu cum bellum contra Syllam pararet, Anconae ob nimiam crudelitatem ab exercitu lapidibus occisus est.

LXIX

THE EXTREMELY dissolute Lucius Cornelius Cinna devastated the republic with the most vicious cruelty. In his first consulship, stopped by his colleague Octavius from making a law about recalling exiles and deprived of honor, he fled the city and, after summoning the slaves to freedom, defeated his adversaries. He killed Octavius and seized the Janiculum. He made himself consul a second and third time. In his fourth consulship, when he was preparing war against Sulla, he was stoned to death by the army at Ancona because he was too cruel.

LXX
(63, 29)

FLAVIUS FIMBRIA saevissimus, quippe Cinnae satelles,
Valerio Flacco consuli legatus in Asiam profectus, per
simultatem dimissus corrupto exercitu ducem interficiendum curavit. Ipse correptis imperii insignibus provinciam ingressus Mithridatem Pergamo expulit. Ilium,
ubi tardius portae patuerant, incendi iussit; ubi Minervae
templum inviolatum stetit, quod divina maiestate serv-
atum nemo dubitavit. Ibidem Fimbria militiae principes
securi percussit; mox a Sylla Pergami oppressus[1] corrupto exercitu desertus semet occidit.

[1] obsessus *op Pichl.*

LXX

FLAVIUS FIMBRIA, the fiercest of Cinna's accomplices, went to Asia as a lieutenant to the consul Valerius Flaccus. Discharged because of dissension, he bribed the army and saw to it that its leader was killed. He himself took up the insignia of command, entered the province, and drove Mithridates from Pergamum. He ordered that Troy be burned because the city had opened its gates too slowly; the temple of Minerva remained undamaged and its preservation was interpreted by all as an act of divine majesty. In the same place, Fimbria struck with an axe the chiefs of the military. Soon he was besieged by Sulla at Pergamum; deserted by his army, which had been bribed, he killed himself.

LXXI
(64, 9)

VIRIATHUS genere Lusitanus, ob paupertatem primo
mercennarius, deinde alacritate venator,[1] audacia latro,
ad postremum dux, bellum adversum Romanos sumpsit
eorumque imperatorem Claudium Unimanum,[2] dein
Gaium Nigidium oppressit. Pacem a Popilio maluit
integer petere quam victus, et cum alia dedisset et arma
retinerentur, bellum renovavit. Caepio cum vincere
aliter non posset, duos satellites pecunia corrupit, qui
Viriathum vino depositum peremerunt. Quae victoria,
quia empta erat, a senatu non probata.

[1] venator *Sop Pichl*. vector *VNfRC* lector *L*
[2] Unimanum *op Pichl*. Munimanum *VNfRLCS*

LXXI

VIRIATHUS, a Lusitanian by birth—at first, because of his poverty, a mercenary; then, because of his swiftness, a hunter; because of his boldness, a robber; and finally a military leader—waged war against the Romans and defeated their commander Claudius Unimanus and then Gaius Nigidius. He preferred to seek peace from Popilius while his forces were intact rather than after a defeat; and when he had handed over some of their belongings and retained their weapons, he renewed the war. Caepio, unable to defeat Viriathus in any other way, bribed two of Viriathus' comrades to kill him as he lay drunk with wine. This victory, since it had been bought, was not approved by the Senate.

Marcus Aemilius Scaurus nobilis, pauper; nam pater
eius quamvis patricius ob paupertatem carbonarium
negotium exercuit. Ipse[1] primo dubitavit, honores petere[2]
an argentariam facere;[3] sed eloquentiae consultus, ex ea
gloriam peperit. Primo in Hispania corniculum meruit;
sub Oreste in Sardinia stipendia fecit. Aedilis iuri red-
dendo magis quam muneri edendo studuit. Praetor[4]
Iugurthae adversus, tamen eius pecunia victus. Consul
legem de sumptibus et libertinorum suffragiis tulit. Publium Decium praetorem transeunte ipso sedentem iussit
assurgere eique vestem scidit, sellam concidit; ne quis ad
eum in ius iret, edixit. Consul Ligures[5] et Tauriscos[6]
domuit atque de his triumphavit. Censor viam[7] Aemil-
iam stravit, pontem Mulvium fecit. Tantumque auctoritate potuit, ut Opimium contra Gracchum, Marium[8]
contra Glauciam et Saturninum privato consilio armaret.
Idem filium suum, quia praesidium deseruerat, in conspectum suum vetavit[9] accedere; ille ob hoc dedecus
mortem sibi conscivit. Scaurus senex cum a Vario tribuno
plebi[10] argueretur, quasi socios et Latium ad arma
coegisset, apud populum ait: "Varius Veronensis[11]
Aemilium Scaurum ait socios ad arma coegisse, Scaurus
negat: utri potius credendum putatis?"

[1] Ipse *Vop* item *NfRCS* Idem *L*
[2] peteret *LSop Pichl.*
[3] faceret *Lop Pichl.*

LXXII

Marcus Aemilius Scaurus was a nobleman, but a poor one, for his father, although a patrician, carried on traffic in charcoal because of his poverty. He himself at first was uncertain whether to seek public offices or become a banker; but his skillful eloquence gained him glory. At first in Spain he earned the corniculum [horn-shaped ornament awarded for bravery]; he served in Sardinia under Orestes. As aedile, he was more interested in administering justice than in exhibiting the games. As praetor, he was opposed to Jugurtha but was corrupted by his money. As consul, he passed laws about expenses and the voting rights of the sons of freedmen. He ordered Publius Decius, the praetor, who was seated as he himself passed by, to get up, and he ripped his clothing and broke his official chair; he decreed that no one should go to Decius to obtain justice. As consul, he defeated the Ligurians and the Taurisci and celebrated a triumph over them. As censor, he constructed the Aemilian Way and built the Mulvian Bridge. His authority was so great that Opimius took up arms against Gracchus, and Marius against Glaucia and Saturninus, because of Scaurus' advice in private. He forbade his own son to come into his presence because he had deserted his post; because of this shame, the son killed himself. In his old age, Scaurus was accused by Varius, the plebian tribune, of supposedly compelling their allies

[4] Praetor adversus Iugurtham *Pichl.*

[5] Liguras *p Pichl.* Liguros *o*

[6] et *om.* Tauriscos *Pichl.* Gauriscos *V†* Cauriscos *op* Gautiscos *L* Bauriscos *N* Gontiscos *RC*

[7] viam *op Pichl.* via *V om. N†RLCS*

[8] Marium *op Pichl.* Varium *V†RLCNS*

[9] vetavit *N†RLop* vectavit *V* vetuit *S Pichl.* vectuit *C*

[10] plebi *Vo* plebis *N†RLCSp Pichl.*

[11] Veronensius *V* Sucronensis *Pichl.*

and Latium to take up arms. Scaurus made this reply to the people: "Varius of Verona says that Aemilius Scaurus forced the allies to arms. Scaurus denies it. Which one do you think should be believed?"

LXXIII
(65, 17)

Lucius Apuleius Saturninus, tribunus plebis seditiosus, ut gratiam Marianorum militum pararet, legem tulit, ut veteranis centena agri iugera in Africa dividerentur; intercedentem Baebium collegam facta per populum lapidatione submovit. Glauciae praetori, quod is eo die, quo ipse contionem habebat, ius dicendo partem populi avocasset, sellam concidit, ut magis popularis videretur. Quendam libertini ordinis subornavit, qui se Tiberii Gracchi filium fingeret. Ad hoc testimonium Sempronia[1] ducta nec precibus nec minis adduci potuit, ut dedecus familiae agnosceret. Saturninus Aulo Nonio[2] competitore interfecto tribunus plebis refectus Siciliam, Achaiam, Macedoniam novis colonis destinavit; et aurum dolo an scelere Caepionis partum ad emptionem agrorum convertit. Aqua et igni interdixit ei, qui in leges suas non iurasset. Huic legi multi nobiles abrogantes,[3] cum tonuisset, clamarunt:[4] "Iam," inquit, "nisi quiescitis,[5] grandinabit." Metellus Numidicus exulare quam iurare maluit. Saturninus tertio tribunus plebis refectus, ut satellitem suum Glauciam praetorem faceret, Memmium[6] competitorem eius in campo Martio necandum curavit. Marius senatusconsulto armatus, quo censetur,[7] dent[8] operam consules, ne quid respublica detrimenti caperet, Saturninum et Glauciam in Capitolium persecutus obsedit maximoque astu[9] incisis fistulis in deditionem accepit. Nec deditis fides servata est:[10] Glauciae fracta cervix, Apuleius, cum in curiam fugisset, lapidibus

LXXIII

Lucius Apuleius Saturninus, a seditious plebian tribune, in order to obtain the favor of the soldiers of Marius, proposed a law which provided that each veteran receive one hundred acres of land in Africa. His colleague Baebius protested, but Saturninus drove him off by inciting the people to throw stones. He broke the official chair of the praetor Glaucia because Glaucia had diverted part of the people by administering justice on the very day when he himself was holding a meeting; he did this in order to appear more a friend of the people. He secretly incited a certain freedman to pretend that he was the son of Tiberius Gracchus. Sempronia was brought into court to give proof of this, but neither by entreaties nor by threats could she be persuaded to acknowledge as genuine this disgrace of the family.

After the murder of his political rival Aulus Nonius, Saturninus, chosen plebian tribune again, granted land in Sicily, Achaia, and Macedonia to new colonists; the gold which was obtained by the guile or crime of Caepio he directed toward the purchase of new land. He deprived of water and fire anyone who did not swear to obey his laws. Many nobles opposing this law shouted out when there was a crash of thunder. Saturninus said: "If you don't shut up, it will soon hail." Metellus Numidicus preferred exile rather than taking the oath. Saturninus, chosen plebian tribune for the third time, in an effort to make his accomplice Glaucia praetor, arranged

et tegulis desuper interfectus est. Caput eius Rabirius quidam senator per convivia in ludibrium circumtulit.

[1] Sempronia soror Gracchorum producta *op Pichl.*

[2] Nonio *Schott* Mummio *VNfRo* Mumio *LCS* Nummio *p* Nunnio *Wijga Pichl.*

[3] abrogantes *VNfR* obrogantes *CSop Pichl.*

[4] clamarunt *RL Pichl.* clamavit *VNfS* clamarent *op*

[5] quiescetis *op Pichl.*

[6] Memmium *Schott* Mummium *VoN Pichl.* Mumium *fRCS* Mimium *L* Nummium *p*

[7] censetur *Vop* censeretur *NfRLS Pichl.*

[8] dent *Vop* darent *NRLCS Pichl.* daret *f*

[9] astu *Arntz* questu *VNfRL* aestu *op Pichl.* gusto *S*

[10] est *om. op Pichl.*

the murder of Glaucia's rival Memmius in the Campus Martius. Marius, armed by the decree of the Senate ordering the consuls to take precautions lest the state suffer any harm, pursued Saturninus and Glaucia to the Capitol and blockaded them. After a very clever trick of cutting the waterlines, he accepted their surrender. Marius' word of honor to the men was not kept; Glaucia's neck was broken, and Apuleius fled to the Curia, where he was killed by rocks and tiles hurled from above. A certain senator named Rabirius carried his head around at banquets for a joke.

LXXIV
(66, 19)

Lucius Licinius Lucullus nobilis, disertus et dives, munus quaestorium amplissimum dedit. Ministro[1] Murena in Asia classem Mithridatis et Ptolomaeum regem Alexandriae consuli Sullae conciliavit. Praetor Africam iustissime rexit. Adversus Mithridatem missus collegam suum Cottam Chalcedone obsessum liberavit. Cyzicon[2] obsidione solvit. Mithridatis copias ferro et fame afflixit eumque regno suo id est Ponto expulit. Quem rursum cum Tigrane rege Armeniae subvenientem[3] magna felicitate superavit. Nimius in habitu, maxime signorum et tabularum amore flagravit. Post cum alienata mente desipere[4] coepit, tutela eius Marco Lucullo fratri permissa est.

[1] Ministro Murenae *op* Miner Murena *V* Mox per Murenam *NfRLCS Pichl.*

[2] Cyzicum *Pichl.*

[3] subvenientem *VNS* subveniente *fRLC Pichl.* venientem *op*

[4] coepit *scripsi* coepisset *Pichl.* cepit *VNfRLCS* cepisset *op*

LXXIV

Lucius Licinius Lucullus, noble, eloquent, and wealthy, in his quaestorship gave the most magnificent public show. With Murena's assistance in Asia, he won over to the consul Sulla the fleet of Mithridates and Ptolemy, king at Alexandria. As praetor, he administered Africa most justly. Sent against Mithridates, he freed his colleague Cotta from blockade at Chalcedon. He relieved Cyzicum from siege. He destroyed Mithridates' forces by the sword and by starvation and drove Mithridates from his kingdom, that is, from the Pontus. Lucullus with great success again defeated Mithridates, who had joined forces with Tigranes, king of Armenia. He was preoccupied with appearance; he was inflamed especially by a love of statues and paintings. When he later went out of his mind and began to act foolishly, he was put into the care of his brother Marcus Lucullus.

LXXV
(67, 9)

CORNELIUS SULLA, in[1] fortuna Felix dictus, cum parvulus a nutrice ferretur, mulier obvia: "Salve," inquit, "puer tibi et reipublicae tuae felix;" et statim quaesita, quae[2] hoc dixisset, non potuit inveniri. Hic quaestor Marii Iugurtham a Boccho in deditionem accepit. Bello Cimbrico et Teutonico legatus bonam operam navavit. Praetor inter cives ius dixit. Praetor Ciliciam provinciam habuit. Bello sociali Samnitas[3] Hirpinosque superavit. Ne monumenta Bocchi tollerentur, Mario restitit. Consul Asiam sortitus Mithridatem apud Orchomenum[4] et Chaeroniam[5] proelio fudit, Archelaum praefectum eius Athenis vicit, portum Piraeum recepit, Maedos et Dardanos in itinere superavit. Mox cum[6] rogatione Sulpicia imperium eius transferretur ad Marium, in Italiam regressus corruptis adversariorum exercitibus Carbonem Italia expulit, Marium apud Sacriportum, Telesinum apud portam Collinam vicit. Mario Praeneste interfecto Felicem se edicto appellavit. Proscriptionis tabulas primus proposuit. Novem milia dediticiorum[7] in villa publica cecidit. Numerum sacerdotum auxit, tribuniciam potestatem minuit. Republica ordinata dictaturam deposuit; unde se[8] receptus Puteolos concessit et morbo, qui phthiriasis[9] vocatur, interiit.

[1] a fortuna *op Pichl.*
[2] quae hoc *VNCop* quae haec *ƒRLS Pichl.*
[3] Samnites *Pichl.*

LXXV

CORNELIUS SULLA was called Felix (Lucky) because of his good fortune. As a very young boy, he was being carried by his nurse when a woman met them and said, "Hail child, lucky for yourself and your republic." An immediate search was made for the woman who had said this, but she could not be found. As Marius' quaestor, he received Jugurtha from Bocchus as prisoner. Lieutenant in the war against the Cimbri and Teutones, he rendered outstanding assistance. As praetor, he administered justice to the citizens and governed the province of Cilicia. In the Social War, he defeated the Samnites and the Hirpines. He prevented Marius from destroying the monuments of Bocchus. As consul, he obtained Asia by lot and routed Mithridates at Orchomenus and Chaeronia, conquered his commander Archelaus at Athens, seized the harbor Piraeus, and on his journey defeated the Medes and Dardanians. Later, when his command was transferred to Marius by the Sulpician bill, Sulla returned to Italy, bribed the armies of his adversaries, drove Carbo from Italy, defeated Marius at Sacriportus and Telesinus at the Colline Gate. At the death of Marius at Praeneste, he conferred upon himself by decree the name Lucky. He was the first to put forth the proscription lists. In the Public Villa he killed nine thousand who had surrendered. He increased the number of priests and re-

⁴ Orchomenum *Pichl.* Orchomenam *omnes codd.*

⁵ Caeromam *Vƒ*

⁶ cum rogatione *ƒRLCSop Pichl.* cum interrogatione *VN*

⁷ dediticiorum *VSp* dediciorum *o* deditorum *NƒRC*

⁸ se receptus *scripsi* spe receptus *VNƒRLCS* sperni coeptus *op Pichl.*

⁹ phthiriasis *Pichl.* thyriasis *V* tyriasis *ƒRLN* tirasiis *C* turalis *S* ptyriasis *op*

duced the power of the tribunes. When the republic had been set in order, he lay down his dictatorship; and then he retired and withdrew to Puteoli, where he died from a sickness called phthiriasis.

LXXVI

(68, 4)

MITHRIDATES rex Ponti oriundus a septem Persis, magna
vi animi et corporis, ut sexiuges equos regeret, quinquaginta gentium ore loqueretur. Bello sociali dissidenti-
bus Romanis Nicomedem Bithynia, Ariobarzanem[1]
Cappadocia expulit. Litteras per totam Asiam misit ut,
quicunque Romanus esset, certa die interficeretur; et
factum est. Graeciam insulasque omnes excepta Rhodo
occupavit. Sylla eum proelio vicit, classem eius prodi-
tione Archelai intercepit, ipsum apud Dardanum oppidum fudit et oppressit, et potuit capere, nisi adversum
Marium festinans qualemcumque pacem componere
maluisset. Deinde eum Cabiris[2] resistentem Lucullus
fudit. Mithridates post a Pompeio nocturno proelio victus
in regnum confugit, ubi per seditionem popularium a
Pharnace filio in turre obsessus venenum sumpsit. Cum[3]
id tardius biberet, quia adversum venena multis antea
medicaminibus corpus firmarat, immissum percussorem
Gallum Sithocum[4] auctoritate vultus territum revocavit
et in caedem suam manum trepidantis adiuvit.

[1] Ariobarzanen *Cop Pichl.*
[2] Cabiris *Aldus* agris *VS* acrius *op Pichl.* argis *NfRLC*
[3] Quod cum tardius combiberet *o Pichl.* quod cum tardius ebiberet
p
[4] Bithocum *op Pichl.*

LXXVI

MITHRIDATES, king of Pontus, born from the seven Persians, had great strength of mind and body so that he could manage six yoked horses and speak the language of fifty nations. While the Romans were at variance with one another in the Social War, Mithridates drove Nicomedes out of Bithynia and Ariobarzanes out of Cappadocia. He sent a letter through all Asia ordering a slaughter of all Romans on a certain day; and this was accomplished. He seized Greece and all the islands with the exception of Rhodes. Sulla defeated him in battle and captured his fleet because of the treason of Archelaus; he routed and crushed Mithridates himself at the town Dardanus and would have captured him if he had not preferred to arrange any kind of peace and hurry against Marius. Lucullus then routed him as he resisted at Cabira. Mithridates afterwards was defeated by Pompey in a night battle and fled to his kingdom; besieged in a tower by his son Pharnaces in a popular uprising, he took poison. When he drank it with little effect because he had strengthened his body against poisons by many previous antidotes, he called back the Gallic assassin Sithocus, who had been sent against him and frightened off by the forcefulness of his facial expression. The trembling assassin was assisted in the killing by Mithridates himself.

LXXVII
(68, 24)

Gnaeus Pompeius Magnus, bello[1] civili Sullae partes secutus ita egit, ut ab eo maxime diligeretur. Siciliam sine bello a[2] proscriptis recepit. Numidiam Hiarbae ereptam Massinissae restituit. Viginti sex annos[3] natus[4] triumphavit. Lepidum acta Sullae rescindere volentem privatus Italia abrelegavit.[5] Praetor in Hispaniam pro consulibus missus Sertorium vicit. Mox piratas intra quadragesimum diem subegit. Tigranem ad deditionem, Mithridatem ad venenum compulit. Deinde mira[6] felicitate rerum in septemtrionem Albanos, Colchos, Heniochos, Caspios, Iberos, nunc in orientem Parthos, Arabas atque Iudaeos cum magno sui terrore penetravit. Primus in Hyrcanum, Rubrum et Arabicum mare usque pervenit. Moxque diviso orbis imperio, cum Crassus Syriam, Caesar Galliam, Pompeius urbem obtineret, post caedem Crassi Caesarem dimittere exercitum iussit. Cuius infesto adventu urbe pulsus, in Pharsalia victus ad Ptolomaeum Alexandriae[7] fugit. Huius[8] latus sub oculis uxoris et liberorum a Septimio, Ptolomaei[9] praefecto, mucrone confossum est. Iamque defuncti caput gladio praecisum, quod usque ad ea tempora fuerat ignoratum. Truncus Nilo iactatus a Servio Codro rogo inustus humatusque est inscribente sepulcro: Hic positus est Magnus. Caput ab Achilla, Ptolomaei[10] satellite, Aegyptio velamine involutum cum anulo Caesari praesentatum

LXXVII

GNAEUS POMPEIUS MAGNUS, following the party of Sulla in the civil war, was especially esteemed by Sulla because of his actions. Without war, he recovered Sicily from those proscribed. He seized Numidia from Hiarba and restored it to Massinissa. He celebrated a triumph at the age of twenty-six. When Lepidus wished to repeal the ordinances of Sulla, Pompey, a private citizen, banished him from Italy. Sent to Spain as praetor in place of the consuls, he defeated Sertorius. Later, he subdued the pirates in forty days. He forced Tigranes to surrender and Mithridates to poison. Then, with wonderful good luck in his affairs, he caused great terror of himself as he advanced among the Albanians, Colchians, Heniochians, Caspians, and Hiberians in the north and the Parthians, Arabians, and Jews in the east. He was the first to reach the Hyrcanian Sea, the Red Sea, and the Arabian Sea. Later, in the division of the empire of the world, Crassus obtained Syria; Caesar, Gaul; and Pompey, Rome.

After the death of Crassus, Pompey ordered Caesar to disband his army but was driven from the city when Caesar approached prepared for battle. Defeated at Pharsalia, he fled to Ptolemy at Alexandria. Septimius, an officer of Ptolemy, stabbed Pompey in the side with a sword in the sight of Pompey's wife and children. The

est; qui non continens lacrimas illud plurimis et pretio-
sissimis odoribus cremandum curavit.[11]

[1] bello civili *VNop* civili bello *fRLCS Pichl.*

[2] a proscriptis *op Pichl.* a om. *VNfRLCS*

[3] annos *Pichl.* annorum *omnes codd.*

[4] natus *om. op C*

[5] abrelegavit *scripsi* fugavit *op Pichl.* abrogavit *cett. codd.*

[6] facilitate et celeritate nunc in septemtrionem *op* mira felicitate
nunc in septemtrionem *Pichl.*

[7] Alexandriae regem confugit. Eius imperio ab Achilla et Potino
satellitibus occisus est. *op Pichl.*

[8] Huius latus . . . cremandum curavit *om. op*

[9] Ptolomi *V*

[10] Ptolomi *V*

[11] *Hic finem faciunt VNfRLCS*

head was cut from the lifeless body; such an action had been unknown before this time. The rest of the body, thrown into the Nile and burned on a funeral pile by Servius Codrus, was buried in a tomb with this inscription: Here lies Pompey the Great. Pompey's head, wrapped with an Egyptian covering, was presented along with a ring to Caesar by Achillas, an attendant of Ptolemy. Caesar could not keep back tears, and he took care that the head was burned with many very costly perfumes.

APPENDIX NOMINUM

Appendix Nominum

Acca Laurentia: wife of the shepherd Faustulus who raised Romulus and Remus.

Achillas: an attendant of Ptolemy at Alexandria when Pompey was killed (48 B.C.).

Achilles: great hero of the Greeks in the Trojan War.

Marcus Acilius Glabrio: consul in 191 B.C.

Acron: leader of Caenina, defeated by Romulus.

Adherbal: ruler in Numidia (118–112 B.C.).

L. Aemilius Paullus Macedonicus: praetor in Spain in 191 B.C., consul in 182.

L. Aemilius Regillus: praetor in 190 B.C., defeated fleet of Antiochus.

M. Aemilius Scaurus: consul 115 B.C., censor in 109 with Drusus.

Aesculapius: god of healing.

Amulius: son of Proca, killed by Romulus and Remus.

Ancus Marcius: the fourth king of Rome.

Andriscus: also called Pseudophilippus of Macedon.

Antigonus: king of Macedonia

Antiochus: the Great, became king of Syria in 223 B.C.

Antyllius: herald of the consul Opimius.

Apuleius Saturninus: plebian tribune; opponent of Furius Camillus.

Lucius Apuleius Saturninus: plebian tribune in 103 and 100 B.C.

Archelaus: general of Mithridates.

Ariobarzanes: king of Cappadocia.

Aruns: son of Tarquin the Proud.

Atilius Calatinus: consul 258, 254 B.C.; took Panormus.

Marcus Atilius Regulus: consul 267, 256 B.C.; captured by Xanthippus.

Attalus: king of Pergamum 138–133 B.C.; made Romans his heirs.

Attius Nevius: soothsayer who cut stone with a razor.

Baebius: colleague to plebian tribune L. Apuleius Saturninus.

Bocchus: father-in-law of Jugurtha.

Caepio: quaestor in 100 B.C.; opponent to Saturninus.

Calpurnius Flamma: military tribune under Atilius Calatinus.

Carbo: leader of Marian party.

Castor: brother of Pollux; honored by Romans.

Celer: centurion who killed Remus.

Ceres: goddess of grain.

Cineas: legate of Pyrrhus, king of Epirus.

Claudia: a Vestal Virgin who moved the statue of the mother of the gods.

Claudius: colleague of Tiberius Sempronius Gracchus.

Appius Claudius: decemvir; desired Virginia, daughter of the centurion Verginius.

Appius Claudius Audax: consul 264 B.C.; defeated Hiero of Sicily.

Appius Claudius Caecus: consul 307, 296 B.C.; rejected peace proposals of Pyrrhus.

Claudius Nero: consul in 207 with Livius Salinator; defeated Hasdrubal.

Claudius Unimanus: commander of Roman forces defeated by Viriathus.

Cloelia: Roman girl, hostage to Porsenna.

Cloelius Gracchus: led Volscians and Sabines against Rome.

Consus: Roman god.

Cornelia: wife of Tiberius Sempronius Gracchus.

Lucius Cornelius Cinna: consul 87, 86, 85, 84 B.C.; leader of Democratic party.

Cornelius Cossus: hero against Fidenates; killed Lars Tolumnius.

Cotta: consul 74 B.C.; defeated by Mithridates.

Crassus: triumvir with Pompey and Julius Caesar.

Gaius Crassus: triumvir with Fulvius Flaccus and Gaius Gracchus for dividing lands.

Critolaus: leader of the Achaians.

Curiatii: three Alban brothers who fought the Horatii.

Marcus Curius Dentatus: plebian hero who conquered the Samnites, Sabines, Lucanians, and Pyrrhus.

Cypselus: tyrant of Corinth (seventh century B.C.).

Decius: plebian tribune who opposed Gnaeus Marcius Coriolanus.

Publius Decius: praetor violated by Marcus Aemilius Scaurus.

Publius Decius Mus: military tribune in First Samnite War.

Decius Mus: sent by Rome to help Vulsinii.

Demaratus: father of Lucius Tarquinius Priscus.

Demetrius: son of Phillip; given as hostage of Quintus Flaminius.

Diana: goddess of the moon.

Dineus: leader of Corinthians against Lucius Mummius.

Gnaeus Duillius: defeated Carthaginian fleet in the First Punic War.

Egeria: the nymph-wife of Numa Pompilius.

Ennius: celebrated Roman poet (239–169 B.C.).

Euphorus: slave to Gaius Gracchus.

Fabii: distinguished Roman family; undertook war with Veii.

Fabius: Roman general.

Fabius Ambustus: father-in-law of Licinius Stolo.

Quintus Fabius Maximus Cunctator: consul, dictator in the Second Punic War, defeated Hannibal.

Quintus Fabius Rullus Maximus: hero of the Samnite Wars.

Fabricius: consul; hero in war against Pyrrhus.

Faustulus: Roman shepherd who raised Romulus and Remus.

Flaminius: consul in 223 and 217 B.C.; defeated by Hannibal.

Lucius Flaminius: consul 192 B.C.; expelled from Senate in 184.

Flavius Fimbria: accomplice of Cinna; committed suicide in 85 B.C.

Fulvius Flaccus: consul 125 B.C.; member of Gracchan Agrarian Commission.

Quintus Fulvius Nobilior: consul; defeated Vettones and Oretanians.

Furius Camillus: saved Rome from the Gauls.

Galba: military tribune, prosecuted by Cato in 149 B.C.

Glaucia: praetor killed by Marius.

Gaius Gracchus: younger brother of Tiberius Gracchus; active in Reform party.

Hamilcar: Carthaginian general; father of Hannibal.

Hannibal: Carthaginian general; son of Hamilcar.

Hasdrubal: Carthaginian general; brother of Hannibal.

Hercules: Greek hero of mythology.

Herennius: father of Pontius Telesinus, leader of the Samnites.

Hiarba: controlled Numidia, defeated by Pompey.

Hiero: fought with Carthage against Rome, later became faithful ally to Romans.

Himilco: Carthaginian general in First Punic War.

Hirtuleii fratres: subdued in Spain by Q. Metellus Pius.

Horatii: three Roman brothers who defeated the three Alban Curiatii.

Horatius: only survivor of the three Roman brothers.

Horatius Cocles: held off the Etruscans from the bridge.

Aulus Hostilius Mancinus: led Romans against Numantia; obtained peace through his quaestor, Tiberius Gracchus.

Hostus Hostilius: hero of Rome; fell in battle against Sabines.

Tullus Hostilius: third king of Rome.

Ianus: Italian deity; a temple to Janus Geminus stood in the Forum.

Iugurtha: ruler in Numidia; defeated by Marius.

Iulius Caesar: triumvir, defeated Pompey at Pharsalia.

Iulius Proculus: noble who settled dispute between the patres and people after Romulus' death.

Iunius Brutus: nephew of Tarquin the Proud; became the first consul.

Iuno: queen of the gods; wife of Jupiter.

Iuppiter: ruler of the gods.

Iuppiter Elicius: surname of Jupiter.

Iuppiter Feretrius: surname of Jupiter, subduer of enemies.

Iuppiter Stator: epithet of Jupiter who makes a thing stand fast.

Gaius Laelius: friend of Scipio Aemilianus.

Publius Laetorius: friend of Gaius Gracchus; defended him against the crowd at the wooden bridge.

Laevinus: consul; led Roman forces against Pyrrhus.

Lars Tolumnius: leader of Fidenates; killed by Cossus.

Lepidus: consul 78 B.C.; tried to repeal the ordinances of Sulla.

Lucius Licinius Lucullus: Roman commander in the East; fought Mithridates.

Licinius Stolo: plebian tribune; proposed law that opened the consulship to the plebs.

Marcus Livius: priest called upon by Publius Decius.

Marcus Livius Drusus: Roman political leader; killed by an assassin.

Livius Salinator: consul with Claudius Nero in 207; defeated Hasdrubal.

Lucan: brave individual under standard of Fabius Maximus Cunctator.

Lucretia: wife of Tarquinius Collatinus; raped by Tarquinius Sextus.

Lucretius Afella: besieged Marius in Praeneste.

Lucretius Vispillo: aedile who threw Gracchus' body into the Tiber.

Marcus Lucullus: brother of L. Licinius Lucullus.

Quintus Lutatius Catulus: Roman commander in First Punic War.

Spurius Maelius: killed by Servilius Ahala; suspected of royal ambition.

Mago: Carthaginian leader; brother of Hannibal.

Magudulsa: prince of Mauritania, killed by Bocchus.

Titus Mallius: Roman commander in Africa.

Mamilius: of Tusculum; son-in-law of Tarquin.

Manlius Capitolinus: held the Capitol against the Gauls.

Titus Manlius Torquatus: killed a Gallic challenger and wore his necklace.

Gaius Manlius Vulso: succeeded Scipio in the East; fought the Pisidians and Galatians.

Marcus Marcellus: consul five times; killed in ambush of Hannibal.

Gnaeus Marcius Coriolanus: Roman leader who captured Corioli; led Volscians against Rome.

Marius Statilius: restrained by Fabius Maximus Cunctator from defecting.

Gaius Marius: consul seven times; fought Sulla in Roman Civil War.

Mars: god of warfare; father of Romulus and Remus.

Massinissa: Numidian leader; became ally to Scipio.

Memmius: rival of Glaucia for the praetorship; murdered by Saturninus.

Menenius Agrippa Lanatus: commander against Sabines; died in poverty.

Metella: sister of Q. Caecilius Metellus Numidicus.

Quintus Caecilius Metellus Macedonicus: consul; defeated Andriscus; had four distinguished sons.

Quintus Caecilius Metellus Numidicus: consul; defeated Jugurtha; exiled and later recalled.

Quintus Metellus Pius: son of Numidicus; as consul fought Sertorius.

Metius Fufetius: leader of Alba, killed by Tullus Hostilius.

Minerva: goddess of wisdom.

Minucius: master of the cavalry under F. Maximus.

Quintus Minucius: consul besieged on Mt. Algidus by Cloelius Gracchus.

Minucius Rufus: plebian tribune who opposed Gaius Gracchus.

Mithridates: king of Pontus, defeated by Pompey.

Mucius: consul when Tiberius Gracchus was killed.

Mucius Cordus: courageous Roman who tried to kill Porsenna.

Lucius Mummius Achaicus: defeated and sacked Corinth.

Murena: legate of Lucullus; assisted him in war with Mithridates.

Nabis: of Sparta; delivered his son as hostage to Quintus Flaminius.

Nicomedes: king of Bithynia; driven out by Mithridates.

Gaius Nigidius: Roman commander defeated by Viriathus.

Aulus Nonius: political rival of Apuleius Saturninus.

Numa Pompilius: the second king of Rome.

Numitor: son of Proca; brother of Amulius.

Ocresia: mother of Servius Tullius.

Octavius (consul): colleague in consulship with L. Cornelius Cinna.

Octavius (tribunus): colleague in tribunate to Tiberius Gracchus.

Quintus Ogulnius: led legates to summon Aesculapius from Epidaurus.

Opimius: consul in 121, foe of Gaius Gracchus.

Orestes: Roman military leader in Sardinia; M. Aemilius Scaurus served under him.

Orgiaguns: king who opposed Manlius Vulso.

Lucius Papirius Cursor: consul, hero in Second Samnite War.

Paullus: consul defeated in 216 B.C. at Cannae by Hannibal.

Paullus Macedonicus: father of P. Scipio Aemilianus.

Perses: king of Macedon, son of Phillip.

Petillius Ateius: plebian tribune, accuser of P. Scipio Africanus.

Pharnaces: son of Mithridates; led revolt against his father.

Phillip: consul in 91 B.C.; opposed Drusus' reforms.

Phillip: king of Macedon in third century B.C.

Pinarii: distinguished Roman family; managed rites of Hercules.

Pollux: brother of Castor; honored by Romans.

Pompeius: Roman commander in Numantia.

Gnaeus Pompeius Magnus: triumvir, defeated by Caesar, killed in Egypt.

Pomponius: father of Numa Pompilius.

Pomponius: friend of C. Gracchus; held off Gracchus' pursuers at the Trigemina Gate.

Pomponius (tribunus): plebian tribune; indicted father of T. Manlius Torquatus.

Pontius Telesinus: leader of Samnite forces against Rome; defeated by Sulla.

Pontius Telesinus: Samnite general; ambushed Romans at Caudine Forks in 321 B.C.

Quintus Popedius: leader of the Marsi; killed by Q. Metellus Pius.

Popilius: Roman commander against Viriathus.

Marcus Porcius Cato: consul, censor, advocated the destruction of Carthage.

Porsenna: Etruscan king who tried to re-establish the rule of the Tarquins.

Postumius: offered gifts to Cn. Marcius Coriolanus.

Aulus Postumius: appointed dictator by Romans in battle with Tarquin and Mamilius.

Spurius Postumius: consul with C. Veturius; waged war with Samnites.

Potitii: distinguished Roman family; revealed sacred rites and was destroyed.

Proca: king of the Albans, father of Amulius and Numitor.

Prusias: king of Bithynia.

Pseudophillipus: also called Andriscus, of Macedon.

Ptolemaeus: king at Alexandria; responsible for Pompey's death.

Pyrrhus: king of Epirus.

Quinctius: compelled by multitude to be leader in attempt to seize Capua.

Lucius Quinctius Cincinnatus: appointed dictator in 458 B.C.; resigned his position after sixteen days.

Quintius: pretended to be the son of Tiberius Gracchus.

Quirinus: name given to Romulus after his temple on the Quirinal.

Rabirius: Roman senator who carried around the head of L. Apuleius Saturninus.

Remmius: colleague in aedileship to M. Livius Drusus.

Remus: brother of Romulus, founder of Rome.

Fertor Resius: first to devise fetial right.

Rhea Silvia: daughter of Numitor, mother of Romulus and Remus.

Romulus: brother of Remus, founder of Rome.

Publius Scipio: father of Africanus Major; consul in 218 B.C., defeated by Hannibal.

Publius Scipio Aemilianus Numantinus: son of Paullus Macedonicus; conquered Numantia.

Publius Scipio Africanus: Africanus Major; victor over Hannibal in Africa.

Lucius Scipio Asiaticus: brother of Scipio Africanus; removed from equestrian status by Cato.

Publius Scipio Nasica Corculum: consul in 155 B.C., ended Dalmatian War.

Sempronia: sister of Tiberius and Gaius Gracchus.

Tiberius Sempronius Gracchus: founder of Popular party; tribune in 133 B.C.; husband of Cornelia; father of Tiberius and Gaius Gracchus.

Sempronius Longus: Roman leader defeated by Hannibal at the Cremera River.

Septimius: officer of King Ptolemy in Egypt; murderer of Pompey.

Septimuleius: friend of Gaius Gracchus.

Sertorius: Roman general on side of Marius; became master of Spain.

Servilius Ahala: master of the cavalry under L. Quinctius Cincinnatus.

Servius Codrus: burned the body of Pompey on a funeral pyre.

Servius Tullius: the sixth king of Rome.

Sithocus: sent to assassinate Mithridates.

Solon: Greek law giver; Romans transferred his laws.

Sulpicius: patrician who married daughter of Fabius Ambustus; dictator.

Lucius Cornelius Sulla: consul, dictator, fought against Marius in Roman Civil War.

Syphax: king of the Moors; opponent of Publius Scipio Africanus.

Talassius: name used in Roman weddings after seizure of Sabine women.

Tanaquil: wife of Tarquinius Priscus.

Tarpeia: Roman maiden who led Sabines into the citadel.

Tarquinius Collatinus: husband of Lucretia; drove kings into exile.

Tarquinius Priscus: fifth king of Rome.

Tarquinius Sextus: son of Tarquin the Proud; raped Lucretia.

Tarquinius Superbus: the last king of Rome.

Titus Tatius: Sabine king who captured the citadel of Rome.

Terentius: found books buried on the Janiculum.

Tigranes: king of Armenia; fought Lucullus and Pompey.

Tricipitinus: helped to exile the kings from Rome; consul with L. Valerius.

Tullia: daughter of Servius Tullius; wife of Tarquin.

Tullius Corniculanus: father of Servius Tullius.

Valerius: priest employed by Publius Decius Mus in the Latin War.

Valerius Corvinus: military tribune who defeated Gallic challenger with the aid of a crow.

Valerius Flaccus: Roman commander who drove Hannibal back; a friend of Cato.

Valerius Maximus: consul with Cornelius Cossus in the Samnite War.

Lucius Valerius Publicola: one of the first consuls in 509 B.C.

Varius Veronensis: opponent of Aemilius Scaurus.

Varro: consul, commander at disaster of Cannae.

Vesta: goddess of the hearth.

Veturia: mother of Cn. Marcius Coriolanus; dissuaded him from attacking Rome.

Gaius Veturius: consul with Spurius Postumius; ambushed by Samnites.

Virginia: daughter of Virginius; rejected advances of Appius Claudius.

Virginius: centurion whose daughter was desired by Appius Claudius.

Viriathus: led Lusitanian rebellion against Rome.

Virdomarus: leader of Gauls, conquered by M. Marcellus.

Volesus: father of Lucius Valerius.

Volumnia: wife of Cn. Marcius Coriolanus; dissuaded him from attacking Rome.

Xanthippus: mercenary soldier from Sparta who helped capture M. Atillius Regulus.

Index